Henry Codman Potter

Sisterhoods and Deaconesses

at home and abroad

Henry Codman Potter

Sisterhoods and Deaconesses
at home and abroad

ISBN/EAN: 9783337369453

Printed in Europe, USA, Canada, Australia, Japan

Cover: Foto ©Lupo / pixelio.de

More available books at **www.hansebooks.com**

SISTERHOODS

AND DEACONESSES

AT HOME AND ABROAD

BY THE
REV. HENRY C. POTTER, D.D.
Rector of Grace Church, New York

NEW-YORK
E. P. DUTTON & COMPANY
713 BROADWAY
1873

Entered according to Act of Congress, in the year 1872, by
E. P. DUTTON & CO.,
In the office of the Librarian of Congress, at Washington.

ST. JOHNLAND STEREOTYPE FOUNDRY,
SUFFOLK COUNTY, N. Y.

TABLE OF CONTENTS.

	PAGE
Prefatory Note	5
I. Introductory	7
II. Report on Woman's Work	17
III. Letters from Abroad	34
IV. SISTERHOODS AND DEACONESSES AT HOME	91
1. Sisterhood of the Holy Communion, New York	92
2. Order of Deaconesses of the Diocese of Maryland	118
3. Sisterhood of the Good Shepherd, Baltimore	152
4. Order of Deaconesses of the Diocese of Alabama	180
5. Sisterhood of St. Mary, New York	205
6. Bishop Potter Memorial House, Philadelphia	210
7. Sisterhood of the Good Shepherd, New York	233
8. Sisterhood of St. John, Washington, D. C.	239
9. Deaconesses of the Diocese of Long Island	255
V. SISTERHOODS AND DEACONESSES ABROAD	271
1. Sisterhood of St. John Baptist, Clewer	274
2. Mildmay Deaconesses' House, London	290
3. Kaiserswerth, on the Rhine	297
4. Sisters of the Society of the Exaltation of the Holy Cross, St. Petersburg	345

PREFATORY NOTE.

THIS volume was mainly ready for the press some months ago, but has been delayed, partly by the pressure of parochial duties, and partly by the desire to make it as nearly as possible a complete history of Sisterhoods and Deaconesses' Associations in the Protestant Episcopal Church in the United States. This it is believed to be; while in the accounts furnished of similar organizations abroad, it is hoped that there will be found an impartial description of societies which, differing widely from one another, are recognized as representative in their character.

Whatever measure of information the following pages may furnish, is largely due to the kind assistance of the venerable Bishop of Maryland, the Rt. Rev. Dr. Whittingham, of whose prompt and generous help, the undersigned desires to make grateful and affectionate mention.

H. C. P.

GRACE CHURCH RECTORY, *New-York*,
  ALL SAINT'S DAY, 1872.

I.
INTRODUCTORY.

THE PRESENT ASPECT OF WOMEN'S WORK.

THE year 1871 marked an important era in the history of women's work. At the meeting of the Board of Missions, of the Protestant Episcopal Church in 1869, the following resolution was, after some discussion, adopted:

Resolved, That a Committee of this Board be appointed, to report, at the next annual meeting, on the subject of the Organized Services of Women, as a most important feature of missionary work.

In accordance with this resolution, the Revs. J. A. Harris and J. W. Claxton, and Mr. William Welsh, were appointed a Committee, who, at the meeting of the Board in 1870, presented a Report, to which were appended the following resolutions:

Resolved, That this Board hereby recognizes the tested value of organizations of trained laity, and especially of Christian women, in prosecuting the aggressive work of the Church.

Resolved, That a Committee of Bishops, Clergy, and laity be appointed by the Chair, whose duty it shall be to consider and report to the next meeting of this Board the best means of associating the organized or individual efforts of women with the missionary and educational work of the Church.

The adoption of the resolutions was in itself an important step. It was a recognition on the part of the authorized missionary organization of the Church, of the value of associated Christian women in the Church's work, and it provided for a still further step. That step was taken by the appointment of a Committee, consisting of the Rt. Rev. A. N. Littlejohn, D.D., Rt. Rev. H. W. Lee, D.D., Rev. H. C. Potter, D.D., Rev. J. W. Claxton, Rev. J. F. Spaulding, Messrs. Wm. Welsh, and Geo. N. Titus, to whom was committed the duty of considering and submitting to the next meeting of the Board, a plan for associating with, and engrafting upon, the present missionary agencies of the Church, the organized, as well as individual work of women.

The report of that Committee will be found next in order among the contents of this volume, and the adoption of the resolutions appended to it, which were acted upon with an unexpected measure of cordiality and unanimity, and without alteration or amendment, at once committed the

Church both to the recognition and adoption of associations of women for work in the Church, in Sisterhoods or otherwise, and also placed its stamp of approval upon the commissioning of godly women for service, in parishes or elsewhere, as Deaconesses.

It has been said, above, that this action marked an era in the history of women's work. It certainly did not inaugurate that work, for it had been widely undertaken long before. Nor did it contribute to its efficiency by defining its methods or limits. Happily, these have been left as free and unrestricted, alike by the action of the Board of Missions of the Episcopal Church, and by its late General Convention, as they were before. But what was widely wanted was the Church's seal of approval, and its definite and hearty recognition, of organizations and associations already in existence. Both Sisterhoods and Deaconesses' associations were at work in different parts of the Church in the United States for some time before the meeting of the Board of Missions in 1871. But they enjoyed, at the best, but a partial measure of confidence or approval, and were looked upon by many sincere and earnest persons, with something of distrust, if not with something more of disapprobation. It was necessary, therefore, that the Church, in its missionary Council, and under circumstances of gravity and deliberation, should put itself upon record in regard to them.

This was the chief significance of the Report which stands next in this volume. There will always be many persons who have serious doubts concerning either Deaconesses or Sisterhoods, and who see in the introduction of such agencies in the Church's work something of danger to her truest welfare. It will be an evil day if such persons are ever denied the right, not merely to hold and defend such opinions, but also to organize for Christian usefulness in those other and less formal ways which such opinions imply. But, meantime, those who do not share their apprehensions, and to whom, diligently reading Holy Scripture and ancient authors, it is evident that from the earliest days of the Church's history there have been such orders and authorized agencies, are entitled to be protected from the imputation that, in striving to revive those orders and agencies among us, they are unfaithful to the Church's Reformed character or distinctive standards. Such protection, the recent action of the Church in her Board of Missions secures to them; and while no particular method or organization is required of devout women willing to work for Christ, such organizations as are described in this volume are placed within the lines of the Church's unequivocal countenance and approval.

In consequence of this recognition on the part of the general councils of the Church, there has been awakened a wide-spread interest in the whole matter of Sisterhoods and Deaconesses' associations, and a very general inquiry as to their modes of organization, and methods of operation. It is the aim of this volume to answer such inquiries. It does not undertake to discuss the general questions as to the scriptural authority, primitive and mediæval history, or general expediency of such associations, all of which have been very ably and abundantly treated of in such volumes as Dean Howson's *Deaconesses*,* Mr.

---

* *Deaconesses,* or the Official help of Women in Parochial Work, and in Charitable Institutions, by the very Rev. J. S. Howson, D.D. London: Longmans, 1862.

Ludlow's *Women's Work in the Church*,* Miss Goodman's *Sisterhoods in the Church of England*,† &c. (to which readers of this volume who may desire to investigate those questions are referred), but rather to afford models of organization and to furnish more particular information as to details of work and rules of government for such persons in our own Church as may desire to labor in and through such organizations themselves, or to set them in operation for others.

For this purpose the following pages include sketches of all the Sisterhoods and Deaconesses' institutions at present in existence in our own Church in this country, together with information concerning the institution at Clewer, England, the "Mildmay Deaconesses Home" in London, and the Training House for Deaconesses at Kaisersworth on the Rhine. Together with these, are forms for the setting apart of Sisters, Deaconesses, and helpers.

The question of the comparative advantages

---

* *Woman's Work in the Church.* Historical Notes on Deaconesses and Sisterhoods, by J. M. Ludlow. Strahan, 1866.

† *Sisterhoods in the Church of England*, with Notices of some of the Charitable Sisterhoods of the Romish Church, by Margaret Goodman. London: Smith, Elder, & Co.

of Sisterhoods and Associations of Deaconesses is not discussed in this volume, simply because it is one aside from its general aim. Whatever may be the various opinions as to this question, (and they will be apt to differ as widely as men and women are wont to differ concerning other questions of method,) it is certainly not desirable that the experiment of associating women with the organized work of the Church, (if at this late day it can be called an experiment,) should be unduly narrowed or hampered by any restrictions as to the mode of organization. Let it only be distinctly kept in view that the American Church has recognized and accepted such organizations as agencies for a higher and more unreserved type of Christian activity, and not as refuges for a merely contemplative pietism,—as enrolling women to be yoke-fellows, not recluses,—workers, not dreamers,—and it can hardly matter greatly by what name they are known, or under what particular form of commission they labor.

As time goes by, experience will probably decide that Sisterhoods will be wanted at some points, *e. g.*, especially in connection with schools, etc., and associations of Deaconesses at others.

That experience, when combined with the light recently thrown upon the scriptural authority for, and primitive antiquity of the office of Deaconess, will surely demonstrate that the revival of that office is indispensable to the fullest and most efficient development of the Church's working powers, and that for want of it, to use the striking but not too forcible language of another,* "The Church has long remained *maimed in one of her hands.*"

Meantime, what is most urgently needed is, that women to whom God has given the desire, and aptitude, and freedom from domestic ties, which are more or less indispensable for this especial consecration to His service, should be brought to recognize the advantages of organized and duly commissioned work, and encouraged to give themselves to it. To this end there may well be, on the part of the clergy and others interested in this branch of the Church's activities, some more general and systematic endeavor than has yet been made to call the attention of such women as are above referred to, to the subject of

---

* Canon Lightfoot on a *Fresh Revision of the English New Testament.* London: MacMillan & Co., 1871.

associated service for Christ, and to invite them, when expedient, to enter upon its privileges and responsibilities. Let it be clearly and distinctly proclaimed that the cause of the Master is waiting for woman's help!

In conclusion, it may not be amiss to offer a single suggestion to those who are committed to the present movement in behalf of the revival among us of Sisterhoods and the order of Deaconesses, and who are perhaps impatient that that revival advances so slowly. The general recognition and adoption of such an agency in the Church's work as that to which this volume refers, amounts almost to an organic change. But organic changes, if they are to be healthy, must not be unduly hastened. There are so many prejudices to be overcome, there are such ample swaddling-clothes of inherited antipathies to be outgrown, that it must needs be some time before this arm of the Church's warfare shall enjoy the confidence which many wise and godly men and women among us, nevertheless, believe that it deserves. Meantime, it will be a happy augury for its future acceptance and usefulness, if those who believe in the commissioned agency of woman in the service of Christ and His Church, shall be enabled to commend that agency to others by the wisdom and moderation and loving consideration towards even the prejudices of others, with which they seek to enlarge and extend it.

II.
REPORT ON "WOMEN'S WORK."

Read before the "Board of Missions," on the evening of October 16, 1871.

THE Committee appointed under the following resolution, adopted at the last annual meeting of the Board of Missions, to wit :

> *Resolved,* That a Committee of bishops, clergy, and laity be appointed by the chair, whose duty it shall be to consider and report to the next meeting of this Board the best means of associating the organized or individual efforts of women with the missionary and educational work of the Church,

Beg leave respectfully to report that they have given the subject thus committed to them their most serious consideration ; and, in seeking for those practical measures toward which it looks, have availed themselves, not only of the wisdom of those of largest experience in connection with woman's missionary or educational efforts among ourselves, but also, as the appendix to this report will show, of the counsel of some of the most successful organizers and administrators of missionary efforts by women in our Mother Church of England, and in other lands.

In approaching the question, "What are the best means of associating the organized or individual efforts of women with the missionary and educational work of the Church?" the Committee rejoice to believe that it is no longer necessary to argue the right of women to participate in such work, nor to participate in it under the obligations and restrictions of organized societies and Sisterhoods. Indeed, to quote the language of a recent Episcopal address,[*] the subject "may be said to have passed through all the stages of inquiry and consideration usually preliminary to practical action." But, "yet very little has been done. The whole subject floats to most minds in ideal vagueness. In the general thought among us it stands out as a beautiful abstraction, about which many fine things have been said and written, but which few have been found willing to endeavor in any earnest way to convert into reality."

[*] Bishop Littlejohn, before the Long Island Convention of 1871.

It is because this Committee believes that the time has come for such misty generalization to end, that it ventures, without further prelude, to pass directly to the question of methods.

(*a.*) It is obvious enough that any extended scheme for enlisting women, actively and practically, in the missionary work of the Church, must take its rise in those various organizations of the Church's life which are already in existence and in operation. In other words, if the Church would utilize the energies of women, she must begin not with some huge machinery, which shall wholly disregard all ties already existing, but primarily, with woman in her parochial relations. The parish must, at the outset, be the awakener and educator in this direction of every soul within its limits, whose dignity it is to share the cares of Mary, and Martha, and Salome.

There are multitudes of parishes in the land where there are missionary societies, in the sense of there being societies to minister to the physical wants of the *hungry*, and *naked*, and *uncared-for*, but there are very few societies or Sisterhoods where the aim is missionary in that larger sense which seeks to carry the whole Gospel,—not the bread of earth without the water of life, nor yet the religious tract without the food for the body, but both together, in a large-hearted, wide-minded effort to rescue and save souls.

And yet the history of missions, whether in our own or foreign lands, demonstrates unanswerably that the power of *woman*, as a missionary, when it has been ripened and directed by warmth of coöperation and wisdom of counsel, is almost incalculable. And, therefore, the Committee would urge as indispensably initial to the successful realization of any extensive plan for enlisting women in the missionary work of the Church, the speedy organization of godly and discreet women in parishes into parochial Sisterhoods; or, where *this* is impracticable, into other less distinctive associations, with the definite aim of seeking and saving the lost sheep for whom Christ died.

As it is, there is, with all our professed faith in organizations of women, a pitiful paucity of results. The Committee cannot believe that this is because there are no women in all our parishes with the unselfishness, the tact, and the genuine love of souls, which are necessary for missionary work, but rather because such women have never had the claims of such *work* distinctly and persistently urged upon them. It is no exaggeration to say that there are thousands of women in this land and in this Church, with the gifts, the leisure, and the opportunities, if they were only shown how to use them, for doing great and blessed service for their Lord. They are bidden to "*give, give*," but what? Money, garments, tracts,—anything and everything, save that which their Lord wants first and most, and that is, themselves,—wholly, absolutely, and unreservedly, in a life and service consecrated to Him and His, forever!

And even what they do give of service or thought for Christ's poor or ignorant ones under our present system, or want of system, they can only give in a desultory, half-hearted, spasmodic way. A woman "living at home is often surrounded by friends and relations who take little or no interest in her attempts at work for the Master," even if they are not annoyed by them. It is not only very difficult but scarcely becoming for *her* to assert the importance of her own voluntary undertakings ; and yet the thoughtlessness of others in making demands upon her time often reduces her to the *necessity* of doing so, if she would not have all her strength frittered away upon trifles, which she rightly feels to be altogether unworthy of her energies.

Even in one's own mind it is difficult to adjust such conflicting claims as those of poverty or "ignorance" on the one hand, and relationship on the other,—very painful to assert engagements to the "physically or spiritually destitute," as a reason for withdrawing from domestic or social engagements. "Modesty and sincerity alike shrink from appearing to attach more importance to one's own wretched dabblings in charity than others are willing to *concede* to them ; and yet there is a sense of sacredness about the obligation to the needy and outcast, which makes it impossible to be easy in throwing aside engagements for their benefit whenever they may happen to clash with engagements of mere pleasure. Such conflicts can never arise in a life planned altogether with reference to works of charity ; and only those who have suffered from them, as have Christian women everywhere, can estimate the value of any well-tried and trustworthy means of escape. To be torn in two directions by the attempt to carry on two different undertakings, or to fulfil two different sets of relation at once, almost doubles the fatigue of each; and from such distractions of mind, organized Sisterhoods, or similar associations, though your Committee by no means hold them to be always and everywhere alike indispensable, do unquestionably offer effectual protection."*

In other words, the Church cannot afford to fritter away one of her mightiest forces, when it can most surely be conserved and increased by wise and judicious organization. And therefore the Committee would recommend the practical adoption of the plan of organized Sisterhoods (*a.*) in our several parishes. What work such Sisterhoods shall undertake, how far they shall be charitable or educational, or both, in their aims, must depend on the fields in which they are called to work, and the unavoidable limitation of means and numbers by which they may be restricted. But many a parish possesses already the germ of an efficient Sisterhood in the Dorcas, or

---

* "The Service of the Poor," pp. 232, 233.

Sewing, or Benevolent Societies, at present at work in it. Let such societies be lifted to the level of something higher than half-social, half-beneficent associations. Let them classify themselves into full and associate Sisters. Let them have a rule of life, and a definite bond of union. Let them be led to recognize their capabilities in carrying on the aggressive and educational work of the Church, and who does not know that multitudes of earnest and godly women, working now timidly, hesitatingly, and therefore feebly, would go forth in a sense of recognized place and definite responsibility in the Master's service, to do for Him and for His Church such a work as our doubting hearts have never dreamed of.

(*b*.) From parochial Sisterhoods (which, it may be well to remark, may be either Sisterhoods connected with a single parish, or, in places of limited population, may consist of any association of women from different parishes) the advance is naturally and inevitably to diocesan Sisterhoods. These, from their more responsible position, should be composed of women of enlarged experience, and of conspicuous aptitudes for missionary or educational work.

They should not only be subject in common with all parochial Sisterhoods to the general supervision and *unreserved inspection* of the bishop, but also in a sense peculiar and exclusive, to his need and call. We have as yet no Sisterhoods in this country available for diocesan work, and yet it must be obvious that, in a land like ours, with its opening and expanding field of usefulness, there must often arise occasions when a community might almost be won *en masse* to Christ and His Church if, at the critical moment, the bishop could command a few devout and judicious women to carry the Gospel into its homes; to open schools; to gather in the young; to organize pious persons already to be found there for Christian work, and thus to form a nucleus, around which a momentary enthusiasm might permanently and healthfully crystallize.

And at this point it is proper that the Committee should urge upon the recognition of this Board, as a very important means of enabling the Church to avail itself of the organized efforts of women, what is known in our mother Church of England as the order of *Deaconesses*. The Committee venture to include in this report the following statement of "general principles" and "proposed rules," drawn up and concurred in at a recent conference in England, by the Bishops of Ely, Chester, Salisbury, Peterborough, and Bath and Wells; and sundry of the clergy of their several dioceses, and communicated to the Church at large by the Very Reverend Dr. Howson, the Dean of Chester, who has so recently and so happily addressed this Board in this place:

I. GENERAL PRINCIPLES.

(a.) Definition of a deaconess.

A deaconess is a woman set apart by a bishop, under that title, for service in the Church.

(b.) Relation of a deaconess to a bishop.

(1.) No deaconess, or deaconess-institution, shall officially accept or resign work in a diocese without the express authority of the bishop of that diocese, which authority may at any time be withdrawn.

(2.) A deaconess shall be at liberty to resign her commission as deaconess, or may be deprived of it by the bishop of the diocese in which she is working.

(c.) Relation of a deaconess to an incumbent.

No deaconess shall officially accept work in a parish (except it be in some non-parochial position, as in a hospital or the like, without the express authority of the incumbent of that parish) which authority may at any time be withdrawn.

(d.) Relation of a deaconess to a deaconess-institution.

In all matters not connected with the parochial or other system under which she is summoned to work, a deaconess may, if belonging to a deaconess-institution, act in harmony with the general rules of such institution.

The bishops above named have also united in setting forth the following " suggested rules :"

(a.) Probation.

It is essential that none be admitted as a deaconess without careful previous preparation, both technical and religious :

(b.) Dress.

A deaconess should wear a dress which is at once simple and distinctive.

(c.) Religious knowledge.

It is essential to the efficiency of a deaconess that she should maintain her habit of prayer and meditation, and aim at continual progress in religious knowledge.

(d.) Designation and signature.

It is desirable that a deaconess should not drop the use of her surname: and, with this end in view, it is suggested that her official designation should be "*Deaconess A. B.*" (Christian and surname), and her official signature should be "*A. B., Deaconess.*"

P. S.—It is desirable that each deaconess-institution should have a body of associates attached to it, for the purpose of general counsel and coöperation.

J. London, G. Sarum,
E. H. Ely, W. C. Peterborough,
W. Chester, A. Bath and Wells.

The Committee respectfully commend these " principles and suggested rules " to the Rt. Reverend the diocesan and missionary bishops who are members of this Board, as furnishing a sufficient outline for the immediate inauguration of similar organizations in their several jurisdictions, to be employed in the more distinctively missionary or educational work of our Church, as need may arise or occasion require.

(*c.*) It only remains to your Committee to recommend, before closing, some more definite forms of organization for that still remaining and not yet utilized capability for missionary usefulness residing in the large class of women who, because of their domestic relations, or for other reasons, cannot ordinarily be included in any scheme for parochial or diocesan Sisterhoods or associations of Deaconesses.

One such form has already been found and most happily tested in the Ladies' Domestic Relief Association, whose branches exist in parishes scattered all over the land. There are bishops and presbyters from Maine to the Gulf, and from the Alleghanies to the Pacific, who can bear testimony to the wise, and tender, and blessed ministries of this modest auxiliary to the Church's missionary work.

Above all, there are missionary homes, all over this broad land, to which its loving and discriminating benefactions have gone, that bless God with grateful hearts, and a courage more steadfast than ever, for its practical assurance of the Church's far-reaching and living sympathy.

The Committee would earnestly recommend that the Domestic and Foreign Committees be authorized, if necessary, to enlarge the powers and the functions of this well-tried and most successful agency for organizing and utilizing the individual efforts of women, by providing that it shall be erected into a Ladies' (or Women's) auxiliary Missionary Society, with branches, as far as possible, in every parish in the land, governed by simple rules, in harmony with the constitution of this Board, and having for its aims

(*a.*) The increase of its funds.

(*b.*) The circulation of missionary publications.

(*c.*) The education of missionaries.

(*d.*) The making, collecting and distributing of articles of clothing for missionaries and their families.

(*e.*) The education of missionaries' children.

This Ladies' (or Women's) Auxiliary Society to have at his headquarters a central Committee, and a special department in the "Spirit of Missions,"—the society to hold annual meetings, where its branches may be represented by delegates duly chosen ; the central Committee to have power to undertake any special work, such as that, *e. g.*, among the Indians, and to control its own funds, and the Committee also to have the right to nominate directly to the Foreign Committee, and, through the bishops to the Domestic Committee. Your Committee would also recommend that membership in the Ladies' (or Women's) Auxiliary Society shall be recorded in New York, and that certificates of membership should be issued on the payment, say, of one dollar.

If some of these suggestions should seem too minute, your Committee would venture to remind the Board that its resolution asks for definite and specific methods, which the Committee have endeavored, as above, to suggest.

In conclusion, your Committee desire to record their indebtedness for prompt and full responses to their inquiries for information in regard to organizations for women's work in other parts of Christendom, to the Bishops of London, Winchester, Salisbury, and the Rt. Rev. Dr. Staley, from Lord Hatherley, the Lord Chancellor of England, Sir Bartle Frere, Miss Longley (daughter of the late Archbishop of Canterbury), the Rev. Berdmore Compton, and the Rev. William Pennyfather of the Church of England. These communications are too voluminous to be included in this report, but it is intended to place them within the reach of the members of this Board, and of our Church generally, in a publication soon to be issued. Each one of them is rich in practical suggestions, and some of them are especially valuable as bearing upon a point which your Committee have been compelled to leave untouched, viz.: the relations of Sisterhoods or other similar organizations to missionary work in foreign lands.

In submitting this report to the Board, your Committee feel that it only remains to them to urge upon the *members* of this Board, and especially upon their reverend brethren of the clergy, the importance of prompt and resolute *action.* If the Church believes in organized

Sisterhoods or associations of women as wise and efficient instrumentalities for doing the Master's work, in the name of that Master let us not hesitate to use them!

The Church has already a Training-House for Women (that in Philadelphia), and organized Sisterhoods in several of her dioceses; but her members have too long and too widely stood aloof from these institutions, regarding them, often, with only doubtful approbation, and, oftener still, with ill-concealed suspicion. It is time that we were done with such half-hearted recognition. Your Committee earnestly urge the reverend clergy in our large centres of wealth and influence, to call upon women who may be unembarrassed by domestic or other ties to give their means, their hearts, themselves, to the work of the Lord. Jesus.

Your Committee also respectfully call upon this Board to put its unequivocal stamp of approbation upon wisely-matured and well-ordered organizations of women, as an agency imperatively demanded in the missionary work.

And with this view, your Committee beg leave

respectfully to submit for the consideration of this Board the following resolutions :

Resolved, That this Board, recognizing the tested value of organizations of Christian women in prosecuting the work of Christ and His Church, hereby recommends that measures be immediately taken for engrafting such associations as may hereafter be organized under the constitutional provisions of this Board, upon the already existing missionary organizations of this Church, whether by the formation of "Sisterhoods auxiliary," or otherwise, in such manner as may be deemed most practical and expedient.

Resolved, That the Rt. Reverend, the Missionary Bishops of this Church, together with the Bishops of Louisiana, Minnesota, Wisconsin, and Kansas, be a Committee to consider and report at —— —— what measures, if any, are practical and expedient, in order to provide for the opening of an institution or institutions in the East, West, North-west, or South-west, for the training of deaconesses for service in the Church's missionary or educational work.

Resolved, That the suggestions contained in this report as to the organization of a Woman's Society auxiliary to the Board of Missions, be referred to the reverend secretaries of the various departments of this Board, with power to mature such organization as may seem to them practicable and expedient, and submit it to the consideration of the Church at large through the *Spirit of Missions*.

All of which is respectfully submitted.

A. N. LITTLEJOHN,
HENRY W. LEE,
HENRY C. POTTER,
J. W. CLAXTON,
JOHN F. SPAULDING,
GEO. N. TITUS,
WM. WELSH.

The report above read was at once accepted, and, after a brief discussion, the resolutions appended to it were separately adopted.

III.
APPENDIX TO REPORT.

FROM THE BISHOP OF LONDON.

FULHAM PALACE, S. M.,
August 28, 1871.

MY DEAR SIR:

Your inquiries respecting Women's work in Missions have reached me, unfortunately when I have no time at my disposal to answer them properly, nor indeed am I competent to give an opinion of any value.

I hope therefore to enclose, in lieu of my own judgment :

1. Letters from the Lord Chancellor on Parochial Mission Women.

2. From the Rev. Berdmore Compton, the Secretary of our Deaconesses Institution, and an active member of the Ladies Association of the " Society for the Propagation of the Gospel in Foreign Parts," for promoting female education in India.

3. From Bishop Staley, lately Bishop of Honolulu, the only Church of England Mission, as far as I am aware, in which is a Sisterhood, as part of its missionary staff.

4. From Miss Longley a daughter of the late Archbishop, who takes a warm and intelligent interest in the employment of Zenana women in India.

I believe women to be *indirectly* most valuable agents in evangelizing the sinful and ignorant at home and abroad; but they are most effective at home, (excepting in the case of school-mistresses,) usually in proportion to their tact and delicacy in abstaining from direct *preaching*, as it were, and in winning by kindness and patience a way for the word in season, the apt passage from God's word, and the simple prayer. Probably the same remark will apply to their work as evangelists abroad.

I do not think that such qualifications can be given or improved by Training Colleges. They are the result of the combination of the love of God in the heart, with that fine tact which is one of God's gifts to women, and which real piety usually quickens and refines.

I do not hold so strongly as many that the organization of women into Sisterhoods is important to increase the efficiency of their work. In my experience, I have seen all *parochial* work done as well by District Visitors, as by Sisters: and indeed some of it, most remarkable work—such as Miss Marsh's among the navvies, and that among the Brickfield laborers by a lady in my diocese, have been done by individuals. For hospital nursing and the like there must be a Sisterhood or Association, because *training* is necessary for preparing for the work, and system in the discharge of it.

I think, however, Sisterhoods valuable as inviting, directing and uniting the coöperation in good works of many who, having no family ties or duties, and no special call to this or that work, might have spent an aimless, useless life for want of impulse or opportunity; and I consider that they should be encouraged on the conditions that they admit none who have home ties and duties, and impose no vow beyond one undertaking that as the sister has not lightly sought admission, so she will not lightly, or without good cause, withdraw. I am not aware of any peculiar danger to be apprehended in connection with the employment of women as missionaries, at home or abroad, in the limited manner described above.

The evil *tendencies* of Sisterhoods are those which inhere in the position of women when separated from the duties, affections and anxieties of home life, intensified, perhaps, by a longing for something to lean on,—vows and rules, however strict, on which to repose the will, and spiritual direction as a rest for the conscience and its scruples, and a fondness for peculiarities of dress, ritual, &c., which fill the void which seclusion from society, with its fashions and little excitements, has left.

These tendencies, though gently discouraged, should not be judged too severely. They are occasional drawbacks in devoted exertion for God's sake and man's good; and at the worst are far better than frivolity and worldly dissipation.

I am ashamed to answer so feebly your inquiries, but I have been overworked lately and have as little energy as time.

Believe me to be, my dear sir, faithfully,

J. LONDON.

I have received also a valuable memorandum by Miss Frere, which I enclose. It is endorsed by her father, Sir Bartle Frere, our highest authority in Indian Mission work.

FROM THE BISHOP OF WINCHESTER.

SHANKLIN, *Isle of Wight,*
Aug. 11, 1871.

MY DEAR BROTHER :

I read your expressed desire that I should reply to your nephew's letter as a command, and he will consider it no slight if I thus answer it to you.

Circumstances have brought the detail of the work of Christian women in Sisterhoods more closely under my eye than under that of any of my brethren in the English Episcopate, and I therefore venture to speak to you of his questions as one to whom the work is familiar.

1. That women are intended by Christ to work in His Church *directly* for Him, appears to me perfectly clear, from,

(*a.*) The life of our Lord in His own Ministry --the Pattern of the Church's work, which is the carrying out of His personal ministry through all time.

(*b*.) From the words of the Epistles. St. Paul's salutations to those who labored much in the Lord seem to me to prove this.

2. That the letter of Scripture warrants their being gathered into communities for this purpose under fixed rules as to age, admission, call and life, see 1 Tim. v. 9, etc.

3. It appears to me that the Gospel of our Lord could not, as dealing with Humanity, but make some such provisions for taking up and perfecting the work of those women whom the hand of His Providence marks off from the engrossing cares of the wife and the mother. 1 Tim. v. 14; 1 Cor. vii. 8, 34, 38.

4. I conclude, therefore, that no branch of the Church is perfectly fulfilling the apostolic precept and example, which is not making provision for the due employment of women's *work*.

5. The idea of the work as a whole is, that women whom God's providence calls to such a life of separation from the ordinary life of the wife and the mother, should especially cherish in themselves the life of Christ, and reveal Him to others.

6. In answer, then, to the first question, I say that *all* the works to which *such* women are devoted, are the works of evangelists ; *i.e.*, whether the work be teaching children, it is not solely or principally the ordinary work of instruction, but the revealing Christ to the child ; or laboring amongst the poor, it is not chiefly for their relief ; or amongst the sick, it is not chiefly as hospital sisters for the relief of the body ; or with the fallen, as the attendants at lock hospitals, merely to heal the body, and mend the morals ; but in each case to reveal Christ to the poor, the sick, and the fallen.

7. This leads necessarily to the second question—none can really devote themselves, *e. g.*, to teaching heathen children, as missionaries, like such women ; and this is one great point of missionary life. The parents are reached through the children as they are in no other way. Thus at this moment the schools conducted in the Hawiian Mission are appreciated more than all the rest of our work. But then there is the life of the Sisterhood to sustain and exalt the school-teaching. Their services, their separation to God, tell directly upon their work ; they are

felt to be not merely eminently successful schoolteachers, but women engaged in mission-work for Christ, and using their teaching powers to carry on their mission.

So it is in our missions from Clewer; whether at St. Stephens, Windsor, under the Bishop of Oxford, or under the Bishop of London in the metropolis, the Sister *is* the Sister of Charity, but she is far more; she is the Sister of Charity because to live to her is Christ, and she can thus tend Christ in His poor.

8. And so we pass on to your other questions. For the Sisterhood life is the secret of this strength. *That* is the centre of the power which supports the spiritual life.

One woman, however energetic, would soon be powerless. The constitution of their nature, which grace has elevated, not obliterated, makes them need sympathy, and that sympathy they find in praying, watching, working, consulting, above all communicating together. Moreover, whilst thus they have more strength, there is more evenness and uniformity in their work. The eccentricities of individual life are corrected by the unity of the common life, the individual life still remaining to color separate action and enable one to do well what could not be as well done by another. The safeguards you ask about seem to me to be these :

1. The allying the whole Sisterhood strictly to the Church. (*a*) Her services ; (*b*) Her obedience ; (*c*) and to Her tone. I have ever found the true obedience of the Sisterhood rise with its saintliness. I believe that the Bishop as a living centre must be felt by the Sisterhood to be God's Bishop set over them and amongst them, and that they *will* yield to him all lawful obedience.

2. I believe that no vows of perpetual obligation ought to be allowed, because, (*a*) I do not think it lawful for us to allow such vows, except where Christ Himself has instituted them, as (*e. g.*) for marriage and ordination. (*b*) I think the permission of such vows involves of necessity the monstrous falsehood of a pope with dispensing powers where they cannot be maintained (*c*) I think that the service, continued not from the fresh spring of a perpetual impulse renewed from ever new love to Christ, but because it was *once* what the heart offered, cannot have God's

blessing; therefore I would on no pretext allow vows of perpetual obligation. But there must be a solemn promise of observance of rules so long as the place of a Sister is retained.

The Mission Sisters being allied to a House as *a centre*, even when they are at a distance from it, is a great guard against eccentricity, self-forgetfulness, disobedience, or the fainting of the spirit.

4. *Safeguard.* Never send out a single sister. *Three* is the least number I would plant out. *Five* is better than three.

5. *Safeguard.* The alliance of daughter-houses with the original house as retaining the one fixed measure for all, is, in my judgment, a great safeguard.

6. The careful training of Sisters through a period of *trial*, as well as discipline, at the central house, is one of the chiefest of all safeguards.

And now, my dear brother, I commend this great subject to your fatherly wisdom and that of your whole Convention, praying you to overlook the errors you may detect in this letter, and to give me the help of your prayers and intercessions.

I am ever, my dear Brother,
Yours faithfully in Christ Jesus,
S. WINTON.

To the Right Rev. the Bishop (POTTER) *of New York.*

FROM LADY HATHERLEY.

31 GREAT GEORGE-STREET, S. M.,
Aug 7, 1871.

DEAR LORD BISHOP:

I must apologize for the delay in my reply to your note, but I hope it is of no importance. Our parochial mission women are not "missionaries," in the sense of "evangelists,"—but as we are very anxious to employ women of religious mind and life, and try to impress on them that the great object of all the *civilizing* influence of their work is to raise the poor to better things than habits of decency, cleanliness, and providence, they must do this by indirect religious teaching.

They are pioneers to the clergy. It is their province to find out un-baptized children, but they report them to the clergyman, that he may instruct the parents as to their duty : and it is the same in any cases of *sin* which they may come across.

They follow his directions as to their reading and praying by the sick and afflicted.

I think their general work is perfectly well described in a letter Lord Hatherley addressed to the *Times*, some while back, (a copy of which I venture to enclose,) and the value of the agency is tested by the numerous applications we receive from incumbents, for its establishment. We are only limited by our poverty ! I also forwarded a summary of their work, which I shall be glad if your Lordship will glance at yourself.

Believe me,
Yours respectfully and faithfully,
C. HATHERLEY.

To the Editor of the " Times."

SIR : I was struck, some time back, by an article in the "*Times*" upon the subject of Almsgiving. The article was occasioned by a letter of Miss Stanley, which brought before the public one of her many works of charity, and asked for assistance in laying up a stock of coals, at moderate prices, to be retailed to the poor in the season when both the necessity for the supply and the price would be increased. Your commentary suggested that it might be better to instruct the poor in exercising provident forethought for themselves. Now, I can so confidently speak of the organization of the above-named association, as promoting very efficiently the prudential education of the poor, that I venture, on an experience of its working for nine years, to ask your powerful aid in making it more generally known.

There is no lack of Christian sympathy in our people. The drowning or explosion of a mine, a dearth of food or a cotton supply, is sufficient at once to open their hearts and their coffers. Indeed this sympathy requires direction and regulation far more than any stimulus. Indiscriminate almsgiving might be easily shown to have occasioned more mischief than lavish expenditure; for the first shilling given to a man who prefers begging for it, to earning it, is the first step towards his ruin; while expenditure, however foolish on the part of the spender, commonly becomes a source of support to the honest and industrious workman.

Now the whole scheme of the Parochial Mission Women's Association is directed towards elevating the lowest poor by their own energy, or, still better, saving the all but lowest from sinking yet lower. They are taught how they may make the most of all their means, however slender they may be. Cleanliness in house and person, temperance, intelligent nursing in sickness, provident expenditure, are within the reach of all: provident saving, within that of many who have but the scantiest resources, or none beyond their labor. Doubtless, model lodging-houses, penny-banks, provident clubs, are excellent institutions in themselves, but they are only facilities. The desire to use them must be generated by living agency. This agency is supplied by the Society whose claims I advocate.

Its plan is very simple. A small number of ladies act as managers. They have the benefit of advice, in matters of finance, or in any difficulty, of gentlemen forming a Committee of Reference. A clergyman desirous of availing himself of the agency, applies to the Lady

Managers, and (if the funds permit) his request is at once considered. He himself selects a Mission Woman, and a Lady Superintendent from a higher class, for his Parish, who must be approved by the Managers, and the organization is then complete. A room must be provided for the purposes after mentioned.

The mission woman is selected from the class among whom she is to work. Her payment is regulated, as far as possible, by her previous weekly earnings, and does not much exceed them. Her duty is to visit, under the clergyman's directions, all who will welcome her, and these soon become the large majority. She gives no alms, but offers instruction and affords facilities by which they may help themselves. She enjoins, and, if needs be, will show them how to scrub and clean their rooms, and what to do in case of sickness, and induces them to deposit with her any money they may be able to lay by for the purchase of necessaries or comforts. She informs them of, and invites them to attend weekly meetings held by the lady superintendent, which lady, having received a loan in advance from the general fund, has a supply of blankets,

AT HOME AND ABROAD. 49

bedding, &c., with Bibles and Prayer Books, which she keeps at the mission-room, and there such women as may be able, meet her and the mission woman for a couple of hours. Materials are then examined and selected, and may be worked upon (many have at these meetings first learned to use a needle and thread), while the superintendent reads aloud for a part of the time, and the clergyman usually opens or closes the meeting with Scripture reading and prayer. No article, made or unmade, is allowed to be taken from the room until the whole of the cost price has been paid.

Now the advantages of this scheme are—

1. The Parish is a definite area to be worked, and, instead of broad-cast, hap-hazard schemes of benevolence, an aim is given, and the effect of the work can be, and is, watched. Returns are required weekly by the managers from the lady superintendents of the number of visits made by the mission woman, the amount of money received, and other work done. Each manager receives these returns from specified districts, and visits the meetings without giving any previous notice. If the mission be not satisfactorily

worked, it is either abandoned or suspended. A mission may be closed for any cause by the managers, on the one hand, or the clergyman on the other, at a month's notice.

2. The mission woman and lady superintendent have their definite civilizing lay-work, and the clergyman is assisted by their co-operation, not thwarted by controversial zeal.

3. The mission women are of the same class as those they instruct. A clergyman or lady superintendent might make many visits without producing the effect desired. They and the poor do not often understand each other, when it comes to be a question of interference with domestic habits and arrangements.

4. The test of this effective teaching is furnished by the returns. In the year 1867, over £7,000 (a portion of it in farthings) was collected from the poor of 130 mission districts. The society commenced its work with six missions, and the deposits in the first year amounted to £85. A steady increase to the numbers of 1867 is a very note-worthy fact.

The testimony to the value of the institution is uniform from the clergy who have experienced its effects. The Archbishop of Canterbury, while Bishop of London, gave it his warmest sanction, and, from the fund which bears his name, annual grants are made towards its support. No distinction is made with reference to any supposed theological views of incumbents who wish for the assistance of a mission woman. The average cost of each mission is £35 a year. The clergyman is expected to guarantee a certain portion of this sum, according to the circumstances of the case. The only items of expenditure are the woman's salary, and occasionally the rent of a central room, the advance loans being repaid as the capital of each district increases. The total cost of management in 1867, was only £180. This cost is mainly incurred by the employment of one clerk, and the hire of an office at 15, Cockspur-street. Scarcely a charity can be named where so much is achieved by so small an expenditure.

Those who know with what despair many a clergyman or district visitor enters a sick room, the window of which is closed, the floor of which is foul with dirt, while the patient possesses neither bed, bedstead, chair, nor table, perhaps no blanket or coverlid, can alone appreciate the transformation that can be effected by a woman in the same class of life as the sufferer, who teaches cleanliness, order, industry and foresight, through the medium of Christian kindness and Christian example.

The Reverend T. J. Rowsell, the well-known incumbent of Saint Margaret's, Lothbury, thus speaks of what he himself witnessed of the working of the agency in question.

"For twenty-five years I have been actively engaged in duties in the East of London; I have learnt to feel the want of this agency, and I have now witnessed its usefulness. It is wonderfully adapted to meet the most urgent wants of the poor . . . . . There is no room in the lowest part of the poorest house into which the mission women do not readily find their way. Every clergyman I talked with, of whatsoever shade of theological opinion he might be, was emphatic about the good done by them."

There are at this time urgent applications pending from parishes in the poorest parts of London and Southwark, none of which can be accepted unless further aid be given to the general fund. Subscriptions may be paid to account of "Parochial Mission Woman Association," at the London and Westminster Bank, St. James's Square; to the Treasurer, the Hon. W. C. Spring Rice; and at the office, 15, Cockspur-street.

Your obedient servant,
HATHERLEY.

31, GREAT GEORGE STREET,
January 27, 1869.

PAROCHIAL MISSION WOMEN FUND.

UNDER THE SANCTION OF THE ARCHBISHOP OF CANTERBURY, THE BISHOP OF LONDON, THE BISHOP OF ROCHESTER, THE BISHOP OF WINCHESTER, THE BISHOP OF EXETER.

The Parochial Mission Women work among the lowest classes of the population in London and other towns, amongst those social outcasts whom the hearts of many are yearning to benefit and who often prove so very difficult to reach. They are themselves poor women, receiving from this association only an equivalent for what they might have earned by the labor of their own hands, in order to set them free to give their time and strength to the service of their neighbors.

Their office is not to distribute alms, nor to act as superiors and teachers, but to win their way to the hearts of those among whom they go, by kindly offices of every kind in sickness, in distress, in degradation, and to lead them upwards insensibly by the influence of a friend, of one who sympathizes with them because she has herself experienced difficulties and trials similar to theirs.

The parochial mission women are not sent into any parish or district, except on the written application of the incumbent of such parish or district; he himself selects the woman he wishes to employ, and she is entirely under his control. In every case a lady-superintendent, also selected by the incumbent, guides and supports the mission woman, presides over the women's meetings, undertakes the charge of the savings collected by the mission women in small deposits from the poor, and provides the articles, clothing, &c., which these savings are intended to purchase.

In 1870 the sums saved by the poor in the small instalments collected by the mission women amounted to £8,927. 11s. 10¼d.

In eleven years (from the beginning of the

work of this association in March, 1860, to the end of 1870) the sum total of the savings thus collected is £54,196. 6s. 2¼d.

165 of these women are now supported by the fund.

The letters written to the *Times* by Lord Hatherley, in January, 1869, and January, 1870, brought some considerable increase of contributions to the fund. Encouraged by this the managers ventured to grant several of the most urgent among the applications which they had received, but they regret to say that in the present winter contributions have come in so slowly, and their funds are in consequence so low, that unless considerable additional support can be speedily obtained, they will be reduced to the painful necessity of withdrawing the mission women from several districts.

They very earnestly entreat for help to avert a step which will cause much distress.

The managers rejoice to have been able to render the mission women of great use in the present prevalence of epidemic disease, by furnishing them, for distribution among the poor, with some very simple circulars on the subject of vaccination and of the prevention of infection, drawn up with a special regard to what is practicable in the crowded rooms of the poor, and at the same time by providing, by a special arrangement, through the lady superintendent, an abundant supply of disinfectants, and especially disinfecting soap, at so low a wholesale price that the poor are learning gladly to take the opportunity of buying it themselves.

Further particulars in regard to the whole work may be found in the reports of the association.

The town clergy, both parochial and missionary, speak in the strongest terms of the value which experience leads them to attach to the work of this agency. Their applications to the fund are urgent, and rapidly increasing in number

FROM THE REV. BERDMORE COMPTON,

SECRETARY OF DEACONESSES INSTITUTION.

THE RECTORY, *Aug.* 12, 1871.
No. 7 Henrietta-street, Covent Garden, M. C.

MY DEAR LORD BISHOP:

The first question asked by the Board of Missions of the American Church is, "How far may women be employed as evangelists?"

In answer to this I would assume, that the word evangelists does not comprehend the office of instruction in schools. Obviously women are peculiarly fitted for the instructing of their own sex and the younger boys in religious knowledge in schools. But confining the word evangelist to less systematic instruction, I would suggest that in a certain province of the work of evangelization, lying between formal preaching and formal catechetical instruction, women are peculiarly useful.

Especially from their superior opportunities of intercourse with their own sex, and from the attractiveness of their unpretending convictions, they can indirectly, and collaterally to the work of nursing, etc., do much of the work of preparing both men and women to listen to more elaborate teaching, and more direct clerical influence.

I believe that many a man is won by the gentleness and practical unquestioning faith of our Deaconesses and Sisters, who would simply turn a deaf ear to a clergyman; and many a woman, callous to ordinary influences, may be gradually restored to feminine softness and humility by frequent intercourse with them.

The second question regards the adaptation of women to such work in foreign lands.

On this point I can speak only from my own knowledge with reference to India.

The Ladies Association for the Promotion of Female Education among the Heathen, (in connection with the missions of the S. P. G.) has for some years sent out Zenana teachers to India and employed others on the spot.

The idea has been to begin with girls' schools, and to keep up the acquaintance with the scholars after their marriage, by visiting them in their zenanas, and teaching them there as private friends.

Admission for Christian influence is thus obtained into the very households of the heathen, which are otherwise firmly closed against it. The teachers of the association are for the most part freely admitted by both Hindoos and Mahometans, who would not of course permit the missionary visits of a man.

I am disposed to think that in this view, the employment of women as evangelists in India is absolutely indispensable, and has hitherto been promising.

The third question, viz., that relating to the dangers of the employment of women in this manner, is more difficult. I imagine that there is no danger to those who are the objects of their ministrations. The only dangers to be apprehended, are to the women evangelists themselves. It might be apprehended that they would become self-sufficient, or ascetic. But I cannot say that in my experience either with the Deaconess Institution of your Lordship's diocese, or with the Ladies Association above alluded to (with the details of which I have been familiar for some years), I have seen these apprehensions realized. Our difficulty is to get the women at all.

I have not found practical difficulty in checking self-sufficiency, and have very rarely found it occur. As a general rule the Deaconesses are quite prepared to act in subordination to the clergy.

Neither have I found any dangerous tendency to asceticism. On the contrary the practical difficulty of the Ladies Association is the frequent marriage of their employées, and the consequent loss of their services.

I remain, my Lord Bishop,
Yours very faithfully,
B. COMPTON

The Lord Bishop of London.

FROM THE LATE BISHOP OF HONOLULU.

CAEN, *Normandy,*
Aug. 23, 1871.

MY DEAR BISHOP:

In forwarding for transmission to the United States the inclosed answers to the questions you received thence, on the subject of Sisterhoods, I will just say a few words on the particular one with which I have had to do.

AT HOME AND ABROAD. 61

An educational staff, for Hawaiian female schools, of *three* Sisters, was introduced into the islands by me, after appealing in vain to those of Clewer and East Grinstead, in 1864, which was in 1867 increased to *five* Sisters. These form two establishments, one at Lahaina, the other at Honolulu. Their educational and charitable labors have been a marked success. Government aid is granted to their schools.

They are members of Miss Sellon's society, to whose generous co-operation I have borne ample testimony. They are under vows of obedience to that lady. She is their "Mother Superior," in the usual Roman sense of that phrase. So long as they choose to remain in the society, they are under her *absolute* control, even to the perusal of every letter they may write, and to their being sent abroad (*e. g.*) to Hawaii, unknown to their parents. Nominally they are subject to the Bishop. At the close of my connection with their work, after strong predilections for Sisterhoods in general, after the most liberal toleration of Miss Sellon's rule, and an admiration expressed publicly for her zeal and devotion, I am constrained to say that facts * have led me to the conviction that the authority of the Bishop, *even outside the society's rule*, is merely nominal ; and that the principles on which that rule is based, are radically unsound, and mischievous in their result on human character,

I am, my dear Bishop,
Yours faithfully,
M. STALEY,
Late Bishop of Honolulu.

P. S. It might be well to send this note, if your Lordship thought fit, with the answers. It explains the grounds of much which I say.

To the Right Hon. and Right Rev. the Lord Bishop of London.

———

Answers by Bishop Staley to the questions on Sisterhoods.

1. *How far may women be employed as evangelists ?*

A. In charitable works, such as visiting the sick and poor, and educating the young, more especially the female part of a heathen or semi-

---

* The facts referred to, I only purpose to bring forward if necessary.

Christian population. They alone *can* raise the character of their own sex, often so fearfully degraded.

2. *If at all, are they adapted in your judgment to such work in foreign lands?*

A. From experience, I may say it *is* possible to find persons fitted for the work. But great devotion, steadiness of purpose, temper, tact, an exemption from domestic and natural claims (which ought always to be paramount), are essential, and above all, an unaffected piety that thinks little of externals, and is most set on imitating our Blessed Lord's example.

3. *Is there a sphere in the Church for training houses or colleges for women, intending to undertake mission work?*

A. Most undeniably there is. Such institutions are a great need.

4. *How far is organization into Sisterhoods, or other similar associations, desirable, in order to the increased efficiency of women's missionary efforts?*

A. Unsystematic, isolated efforts can never succeed like organization. Short of the higher motives, nothing aids in a cause like *esprit de corps.* My own experience was this. Schools carried on by earnest women not under organization, up to 1864, had failed from want of stability. Their conductors could be depended on only for a year or two, and the natives ceased to believe in our permanence. They did not care to send their children, as they would soon change their instructors again.

Under organized direction, since the Sisters arrived (none of whom have left in seven years), the schools have been a great success.

5. *Will you suggest any particular plan for utilizing the peculiar aptitudes of women for mission work, if in your judgment such aptitudes exist, and if such a plan has occurred to you; and will you add any general conclusions which you have reached on the whole subject?*

A. Women under preparation for mission work, at home or abroad, should be formed into an Order with a name suitable to their vocation, under certain rules for the due discharge of their office, as well as for the guidance of their inner life. After entering on their work they should continue in that Order under those rules. I deprecate vows, whether for a term, or for life.

But there should be an understanding that allowing for reasonable contingencies, the candidate is entering on the work as the business of her life. In selecting candidates it should be taken into consideration whether any one has a clear call to stay at home, from family or other reasons.

Our Blessed Lord, who on the cross commended His mother to the beloved disciple, does not sanction a daughter's breaking an aged mother's heart, even to do what she believes to be His work, when her presence at home is a comfort, or at least a necessity to that parent.

A board of examiners should be appointed by the Bishops, to ascertain the fitness of candidates as to age, circumstances, qualifications, according to the special work for which they are intended, whether it may be the lower or higher branches of education, or the work of *Sœurs de Charité*. Such persons should have no pecuniary interest in the success of the institutions which they may establish in their missionary field. "Having food and raiment they should be therewith content," and even feel it to be a privilege to contribute of their own substance. Any profits should go to the maintenance of the mission cause. A simple, but not eccentric dress, should be adopted by the order.

The Order and the institution, where candidates are prepared, should be under the presidency of some wise, moderate, experienced lady, one who will rule well as the head of a household, not as "lording it over God's heritage." The rules as to exercises, devotional or disciplinary, should not be oppressive, but consistent with the forms and spirit of our Reformed Church. The same remarks apply to any branch of the Order sent out. Each should be under a *Superintending Sister*, who will carry out the ideas learned at home, who will set an example of quiet subjection to authority herself, and who will not avail herself of the larger liberty she may enjoy, to enter into the gossip of the place.

This reminds me that it is a *sine qua non* that the Order at home or abroad be subject to the Bishops, not as a despot, but as administering the rule and regulating the works undertaken. It is this alone, history shows, which can prevent abuses in societies having in them anything of a conventual character. Each institution may, or may not have a chaplain. But if they have, he will himself act under the Bishop as if he were over a parish. I may add that practices as regards dress, insignia, phraseology, behavior in worship, alien to the Anglican Church, should be discountenanced.

6. *What are the dangers to be apprehended?*

A. This I have reserved for consideration last, because from the cautions laid down already, they may be gathered by implication. I will only add we must seek to benefit by the lessons gathered from the history of all such Societies.

ANSWERS FROM MISS LONGLEY.*

Q. 1. *How far may women be employed as evangelists?*

A. As teachers in day-schools; mistresses of boarding-schools for high-caste girls, and as teachers in Zenanas. In all cases under the direction and control of the president missionary.

* Daughter of the late Archbishop of Canterbury.

Q. 2. *If at all, are they adapted, in your judgment, to such work in foreign lands ?*

A. Particularly so in India, amongst Hindoo females of the upper class, who can only be reached by home teaching in the Zenanas. Efforts already made have proved that the agency of female teachers is most effectual in thus commending the practice of Christianity, and such teachers are earnestly desired, and warmly greeted in many Zenanas.

Q. 3. *Is there a sphere in the Church for training-houses or colleges for women intending to undertake mission work ?*

A. If the resident missionary be a married man, the female teacher should live in the mission-house, and work, if possible, with the missionary's wife.

If this plan is not practicable, and the missionary is not married, a mission-house for female teachers should be established, where two or more may live together; one acting as the head, and directing those associated with her. The work in either case to be done under the guidance of the missionary. There is an advantage in the *latter* plan, that a permanent establishment is founded for mission work, and the system suffers little when one of the body is removed from any cause, her place being refilled.

The plan adopted in England by the Society for the Propagation of the Gospel for carrying out such work abroad, is the best that suggests itself to me, and may be seen by reference to the paper annexed. The members of the association, of every rank of life, are expected to make a personal effort to promote Christian education amongst the female heathen, either by subscribing according to their ability to send out workers, or by offering themselves as candidates.

The formation of corresponding committees abroad, has been found of the most practical utility.

LADIES' ASSOCIATION FOR THE PROMOTION OF FEMALE EDUCATION IN INDIA AND OTHER HEATHEN COUNTRIES,

In connection with the Missions of The Society for the Propagation of the Gospel.

The Ladies' Association has been formed in connection with the Society for the Propagation of the Gospel in Foreign Parts. Its object is to promote female education among the heathen. No heathen country to which the missions of that society extend will be excluded from its operations.

As a testimony to the greatness of the want which the association will endeavor in some degree to supply, the following facts concerning one country are submitted for consideration. The whole number of native girls in India, who are of a suitable age to be placed under instruction, is stated at 16,000,000; the number at school in 1861, was reckoned at 13,000 Christian girls, and 8,000 heathen. In the presidency of Madras, with a population of 26,000,000, the day-schools in connection with the Society for the Propagation of the Gospel include only 1,215 native girls, and the boarding-schools only 265. Yet these boarding-schools, in which suitable wives for native Christians are trained up, are described by eye-witnesses as "one of the most satisfactory branches of missionary education:" and a girl may be boarded, clothed, and taught, for about 3*l*. 10*s*. or 4*l*. per annum. For Hindoo females in the upper classes who cannot be induced to attend public schools, a quiet system of home education, called Zenana-missions, has been recently tried with the most encouraging results.

The association proposes not to relieve any existing society of work which is now being carried on; but to extend the inadequate means of education, by sending out and supporting additional female teachers for native women and girls in different social ranks, by aiding in the support of boarders in native schools, and by helping in other ways the cause of female education. Experience proves that the agency of female teachers is most acceptable and most effectual in commending to their own sex the usages of a higher civilization and the practice of Christianity.

In every parish of our own country, and especially in those parishes in which there is a branch of the Society for the Propagation of the Gospel, it is desired to establish a Branch Association, the members of which, in every rank of life, shall make a personal effort to promote the Christian education of their heathen sisters, by subscriptions according to their ability; by collections from friends; by meeting together periodically in working-parties; by acquiring and imparting information derived from such publicatians as the *Mission Field*, *Gospel Missionary*, *Net*, etc.; and by frequent prayer. An annual subscription of 2s. 6d. or more constitutes a member of the association; and it is hoped that in every parish, some one person at least may be found willing and able, acting as local secretary, to influence Christian neighbors to enrol themselves members, and to join together in this good work. In any parish where a Branch Association is formed, persons willing to become members may send their names and subscriptions to the clergyman of the parish, or to the secretary of the Branch Association, who is requested to transmit the collection and list of names to the office of the society. Or any person willing to become a member may write direct to the Hon. Secretary, 5 Park Place, St. James's-street, London, S. W.

Local secretaries and members who wish to form a working-party, or to receive papers to assist them in collecting subscriptions, or to procure publications connected with the objects of this association, or to be supplied with instructions as to the kinds of work, articles of dress, etc., which are most in request abroad, or to be informed respecting schools in heathen countries at which a native child may be supported, are invited to write on these subjects to the Hon. Secretaries.

CONSTITUTION OF THE ASSOCIATION.

1. That a Ladies' Association be formed for Promoting the Education of Females in India and other heathen countries, in connection with the missions of the Society for the Propagation of the Gospel.

2. That its objects be: (1) to provide female teachers for the instruction of native females in such countries, by supporting abroad, and select-

ing and preparing in this country, persons well qualified for the work; (2) to assist female schools by providing suitable clothing and school materials, and a maintenance for boarders; (3) to employ other methods which may be suggested of promoting female education; (4) to assist generally in keeping up an interest in the work of the society.

3. That funds be raised not only by means of ladies' work, for the sale of which abroad arrangements will be made by this association, but also by establishing auxiliary associations throughout the country for collecting subscriptions, etc.; care being taken in every instance that no association shall divert or interfere with subscriptions to the Society for the Propagation of the Gospel.

4. That, with a view to encourage the accession to this association of members who already contribute to the Society, an annual subscription of 2s. 6d. shall be held sufficient to constitute a member, though larger subscriptions will be thankfully received.

5. That, inasmuch as it ought to be specially remembered that a work of this kind cannot

prosper without an abundant blessing from Almighty GOD, the members of this association be requested to make its success a subject of frequent prayer; and that a short selection of suitable prayers be drawn up for the use of members at their discretion.

BYE-LAWS.

1. The business of the association shall be carried on by a Committee, consisting of the President and Vice-Presidents of the association, twenty other ladies elected from the members, two Secretaries, and two members of the Standing Committee of the Society for the Propagation of the Gospel, with the Secretary of the Society.

2. The ordinary meetings of the Committee shall take place on the second Wednesday in each month at 11 A.M., except the months of August and September. Three ladies are requisite to constitute a meeting.

3. The President and Vice-Presidents shall be elected at a monthly meeting, and shall remain in office so long as they continue to be members of the association.

4. Of the twenty elected members of the Committee, the two who have attended its meetings in the past year least often shall retire, and two new members shall be elected in their place at the monthly meeting in May. If under this rule any doubt should arise as to the retiring members, it shall be determined by lot. At that meeting it shall be the privilege of any member of the association to attend and to vote on the election. Any vacancy in the Committee occurring at other times may be filled up at any monthly meeting of the Committee.

5. At the monthly meeting in May, the Committee shall appoint sub-Committees on Organization, Finance, Candidates, and Work and Clothing, who may associate other members with themselves. Other sub-Committees for special objects may be appointed at any time by the Committee.

6. Annual subscribers of 2s. 6d. or more, are members of the association.

7. Annual subscriptions are due on January 1st. All names, subscriptions, collections, etc. intended for insertion in the Annual Report, must be sent in before December 1st.

8. All orders for payment shall be signed by a Secretary and a member of the Committee, under the authority of a resolution of the Committee.

9. The Secretaries shall convene meetings of the Committee; keep minutes of their proceedings; conduct the correspondence of the Committee; prepare the Annual Report and other publications, and superintend their circulation; assist in the organization of district associations; and generally act under the instructions of the Committee.

FROM MISS FRERE,

ENDORSED BY SIR BARTLE FRERE.

1. *How far may women be employed as evangelists?*

A. I should say as far as their health will stand the work. They will be found very valuable auxiliaries to established work—and in some cases useful pioneers where work has been commenced.

2. *If at all, are they adapted in your judgment to such work in foreign lands?*

A. Most certainly. The effective work accomplished through such agency by the Church of England (by means of the "Indian Female Normal School, and Instruction Society," in connection with the Church Missionary Society, and of the "Ladies Association for the Promotion of Female Education among the Heathen," in connection with the Society for the Propagation of the Gospel,) by the Established Church of Scotland—by the Free Kirk, the Baptists, the Wesleyans, the Congregationalists, the American Dissenters, the German Reformed Church, and the Roman Catholics, and others, prove this beyond a doubt.

3. *Will you suggest any particular plan for utilizing the peculiar aptitudes of women for mission work, if in your judgment such aptitudes exist, and if such a plan has occurred to you; and will you add any general conclusions which you have reached in regard to the whole subject?*

A. I would venture to begin by mentioning a few general conclusions on this subject, and then endeavor to state one or two particular methods by which the object aimed at seems to be most readily secured.

Women will undoubtedly be found useful auxiliaries to mission work, wherever a settled mission has been established in a tolerably good climate.

On account of health they should not go out too young to such work. Between twenty and thirty years old is the best age—but nearer twenty than thirty.

They should be ladies by birth and education, and it will be found better that they should have some knowledge beforehand of the requirements of those who would teach others, and also of the trials and difficulties of such work. They will also need some facility for learning languages.

In India, which is the widest of the *accessible* fields for mission work, (for China cannot be called accessible to foreigners in the way India is,) the services of women will be found advantageous in three ways:

1. The establishing and teaching in missionary schools—especially girls' schools.

2. In establishing and superintending orphanages.

3. In visiting native women at their own houses, or " zenanas," and instructing them there.

It is not necessary to say that at a prosperous mission, where the staff of workers is sufficiently large, all three branches of this three-fold work may be undertaken, and each branch will be found to assist the others. Access will be gained to the parents through the children, and to the children through the parents — and orphans brought up in the Christian faith will, when grown up, form the nucleus of a Christian colony, capable of sending out in time trained native teachers.

The masses of India cannot, I think, be evangelized until a vigorous native Missionary Church is established in the country. It is at the establishment of this that all missionary work should especially aim.

There are two methods of employing the services of women in mission work. The one, that adopted by the Roman Catholics; the other, that of the Presbyterians. Both systems are good, and both might be employed by a Missionary Church without inconsistency, as circumstances permitted or favored the one plan or the other.

The Roman Catholic method is the establishment of Sisterhoods, each under a lady superintendent; who is responsible for the management of the schools under her charge to the bishop of the diocese, and to the order to which she belongs.

The first thing generally done is to establish an orphanage, with schools attached.

In addition to the primary education given to the orphans, two Sisters, for a small sum from the parents, take boarders and day-scholars; children of middle-class, half-castes, and Europeans, to whom they give what may be called a *secondary* education, a little in advance of that given to the orphans. They also take as day-scholars or boarders, the children of gentlemen, who, though unable to afford the expense of sending their children to England to be educated, can yet afford to pay for an education somewhat better than the *secondary*.

These three classes of scholars are kept distinct in the schools, and the sums paid for the education of the second and third classes, helps to mitigate the expense of the orphans for whom nothing is paid.

The children attending, are all Christians.

Schools for the heathen, and Zenana work, may be taken up in connection with the orphanage work, if the staff of workers is large enough.

The advantage of the Sisterhood system is, that the work does not fluctuate to the same extent as where all depends on the individual exertions of one or two ladies, who may fall ill and be obliged to leave the country, at which their work itself ceases. In the Sisterhood system, a gap is at once filled up. It has the strength of a trades-union, and the perpetuity of a "company."

In the event of the American Church meditating such work by such means, I would observe, this system can only be effective worked in, or near large towns, such as Calcutta, Bombay, Poona, etc., where the number of Europeans congregated will provide a constant supply of *paying* scholars.

The establishment should be under episcopal guidance, or such deputy as the Bishop may see fit to appoint.

The ladies should be careful not to adopt fantastic dresses or names, or any devices by which they could possibly be mistaken by the natives for Roman Catholics; and it would be well that the head of the establishment should be a widow lady, and not an unmarried person, and that she should have experience in the government of a household.

The method pursued by the Scotch and other churches is to send one or two ladies to any mission station, where it can be managed, to live with the missionary and his wife, and assist them in establishing schools and orphanages, and in visiting in the Zenanas. The ladies being under the orders of the missionary, and answerable, like him, to the society which sends them out. This system has also been found to work well, and is less expensive than the other. It is pursued by the S. P. G., and the C. M. S.

With regard to the qualifications of candidates for such work, the agreements made with them, salaries, etc., I would refer to the papers on the subject published for the use of applicants by the "Ladies Association in connection with the S. P. G.," merely mentioning that the ladies belonging to this society engage to go abroad for three years, and if they do not remain for this time (save for the cause of ill-health), they return their passage money; and that the usual salary is about £120. per annum—but this varies with the difference of the expense of living in different places.

It usually takes one year for a lady to learn the language sufficiently to be an efficient teacher in it, and during that time she usually occupies herself teaching those scholars who know English, and otherwise assisting her fellow-workers in various ways.

Ladies should in no case be sent to do missionary work before a mission is established, and a home prepared for their reception; and I would suggest, that where after three years health fails, and yet there is no wish to relinquish the work, leave of absence should be granted for return home and rest, accompanied by a small salary during the time of absence.

With regard to Zenana teaching, the ladies should go emphatically and avowedly as Christian teachers, and refuse to go where they will not be permitted to read the Bible.

There might be great danger from the over zeal of Christian teachers, who, being willing to enter Zenanas without this provision, or declaration, endeavored to smuggle their opinions into the houses they visited, against the plain teaching of Christianity, and thereby might bring Christianity itself into disrepute. Two little books, called "Peep of Day," and "Line upon Line," have been found most useful in India, as an introduction in Zenanas to the study of the Bible.

From the superior facilities ladies have of gaining access to the ladies of heathen countries, they will, I think, always be found particularly valuable auxiliaries to mission work.

MARY FRERE,
Member of the Committee of the Ladies' Association, in connection with the S. P. G. for 1871.
London, 1871.

I concur in the views expressed in this paper, which seem to me sound and practical.

BARTLE FRERE.
August 2, 1871.

FROM THE BISHOP OF SALISBURY.

Aug. 30, 1871.

My Dear Dr. Potter:

It has been a great mortification to me to feel that, owing first to much engagement, and for the last three weeks to ill-health, I have been quite unable to attend to the subject of your kind letter, and to reply to the questions which you enclosed. I write now very shortly, and I am sorry to think very tardily, to say that in fact I have very little to say, and very little power of saying that little.

Direct employment as an evangelist, I own, seems to me to be quite unsuitable for a woman. I mean that actual, express missionary work appears to me to belong exclusively to men, and to be forbidden to women under the general principle laid down by St. Paul in the Epistle to the Corinthians. But having said this, I hasten to add that in hundreds of supplementary ways the aid of women in aid of the direct work of evangelizing, seems to me to be invaluable, nay, to be indispensable. The example of pure-minded Christian women, their delicate tact in teaching and explaining, their womanly skill and tenderness in nursing, their motherly care of little ones, their knowledge and sympathy in regard to their own sex, their gentle influence with men, their humanizing companionship with the actual missionaries, these and a multitude of other things which might be mentioned, render women, Christian, devoted, well-trained women, of unspeakable value in the second degree to a well-ordered and constituted missionary body. But it seems to me that they require to be under the general direction of wise *men*. I have learned to fear female *rule*, unless it be itself under authority, able to know all and capable of controlling or overruling.

I am extremely ashamed of sending you these crude and hasty words; and still more ashamed to think that they will reach you later than the prescribed time. Their want of value is some little diminution of my regret on the second ground. I beg you will present my very kind and brotherly regards to your excellent uncle the Bishop. It is a matter of great regret to me that my age, and poor health, added to my constant work, render it impossible for me to accompany my good brother, Bishop Selwyn, to the Convention in October.

 Believe me, my dear sir,
  Your very faithful servant,
    GEORGE SARUM.

FROM THE REV. WILLIAM PENNE-FATHER.

HAMBURG, *Germany,*
Aug. 9, 1871.

MY DEAR SIR:

Your letter of the 18th inst. has followed me to this place, where I have been ordered for my health.

The subject of women's work in the Lord's vineyard has for many years occupied my thoughts, and we have had for upwards of eleven years a Home, into which we have received ladies of whose piety and earnest zeal we have been assured. Had I been at home I could have sent you some printed details of the work the Lord has given us to do, and if permitted to return to London, I shall hope to forward such documents to you.

We have at Mildmay Park, London, a central house in which our female workers reside, and from whence they go forth by day into different parts of the great city to labor among the sick and those who are "out of the way." We have likewise a house in which trained nurses reside when not actually attending cases of illness. These latter have been very constantly engaged during the past autumn and winter in attending small-pox and scarlet fever patients. God has protected them, and our hearts are very full of praise for His goodness towards them.

I do not think the importance of employing pious and intelligent women in direct work for our Lord and Master can be over-estimated. It is evident that in our Lord's life-time such ministered unto Him, and that in the very early days of Christianity their labors tended to the furtherance of the Gospel. All false religions tend to degrade woman. The Gospel of God's grace raises her to her original position as a real help to the other sex. God sends *man and woman* out into His vineyard, hand in hand, to labor in the blessed work of " binding up the broken in heart," and it seems to me that it requires the strength of the one and the skilful tenderness of the other to effect the work. In our Divine Master (the perfect One) there was united the perfections of the one and the other.

Believe me to remain, my dear sir

Yours most truly,

WILLIAM PENNEFATHER.

IV.

SISTERHOODS AND DEACONESSES AT HOME.

THE following narratives and statements will best speak for themselves. They have been derived in almost every instance from those most directly interested in the Associations which they describe, and the aim has been, as far as possible, to let each body of Christian workers tell its own story.

Of course, under such circumstances, there will be found to be a wide difference in the opinions expressed in the following pages concerning the principles and methods under which women should be associated. No effort has been made to obliterate the traces of such variety of opinion, nor can it be desirable, in such a work as this, that there should be. It would be easy to reduce the whole aspect of the subject to a narrow and monotonous range and tone, but to do so would be to defeat the very aim with which this volume was begun, viz., to present, as far as possible, every practical view of that general movement to which it relates.

As will be seen, the sketches of the American Sisterhoods and similar associations that follow, are arranged in the order of their organization.

1.
The Sisterhood of the Holy Communion, New York.

ORGANIZED A.D. 1845.

THE Sisterhood of the Holy Communion, so called from the church under whose first pastor it originated, dates its existence from the year 1845. It was thus the first Protestant association of the kind in this country, and anterior also to the first of the English Sisterhoods—Miss Sellon's, which did not exist until 1848. The community was regularly organized in 1852, and in the spring of 1853 the corner-stone was laid of the Sisters' House, adjoining the Church of the

Holy Communion. This house was built by Mr. John H. Swift, who thus showed his faith in such institutions among Protestants, while public feeling was strongly against them. The ground on which the house stands was given by Mrs. M. A. Rogers. The Sisters at this time were employed in parochial work, among the poor, and in teaching the parish school. On removing into the Sisters' House in February, 1854, they opened an Infirmary in that and the house adjoining, which was the germ of St. Luke's Hospital. In 1855 they added a Dispensary, which, with the before-named works, occupied the community until the year 1858, when they took charge of St. Luke's Hospital.

In April, 1863, three of the Sisters and one probationer left St. Luke's Hospital and subsequently formed themselves into the "Sisterhood of St. Mary's." The increase of Sisters in the Hospital permitted, in 1866, a resumption of a part of their original work, in teaching the parish school and visiting the poor of the Church of the Holy Communion.

The views and convictions out of which the Sisterhood of the Holy Communion took its rise will best be shown by the following questions and answers, which we are permitted to take from a little work called *Evangelical Sisterhoods*, published under the auspices of the Rev. Wm. A. Muhlenberg, D.D., the venerable Pastor of St. Luke's Hospital, New York, and the founder of St. Johnland.

Question 1. How best may the work of organizing a Sisterhood be begun? If, *e. g.*, a parish clergyman desires to have a Sisterhood, what is the first step?

Answer. No clergyman can begin such a society, though he may prepare the way for it by using his gift as a preacher; he may also foster and employ it after it has come into being, but he cannot create it. Nor can money make Sisterhoods, as some suppose who look upon them as so many asylums for the unprovided, the world-worn, and the world-weary, instead of the households of fresh loving hearts, strong in all their powers to "serve the Lord with gladness," which they ought to be. Neither can conventions and committees begin Associations of the kind; they may advocate them wisely and well, and do good by familiarizing us with the idea, and showing the necessity of embodying it in action, but they cannot originate this action.

Question 2. With whom, then, can it begin?

Answer. With some experienced, believing woman, roused to a deeper sense of her responsibilities as the handmaid of the Lord, and of force of character enough to inspire one or two others to aid her in carrying out her convictions. Such an one would soon find work of the right sort to her hand, and though she had at first but one companion, they two would form a nucleus around which others would gather, the leaven would go on leavening, and gradually there would be developed an effective Sisterhood.

This first or principal Sister must form the heart of the organization; she is the centre around whom the others are to rally, carrying out her directions and deriving through her, in return, supplies, protection, and all needful provisions for their comfort. Referring again to the proposed term of engagement, the question arises, shall her administration be limited to a period of three years? Rather not, I should say. Because every year, as it adds to her experience, adds to her value both to the Community and to the work they may be engaged in, and she could not withdraw without much disturbance and loss to the whole. She should therefore continue to fill her place as long as she is wanted, or until she has trained a successor, or until, in the multiplication of such societies, another is found from among their ranks qualified to be her substitute.

Question 3. What is the simplest and most readily practicable plan upon which to frame such an Association?

Answer. In attempting, as succinctly as possible, to reply to this question, it should be premised that in each community so formed, the details will necessarily be modified by the character of the work undertaken and by the attainments and resources of the Sisters who undertake it. The following would be the general plan:

1. The Association or Sisterhood would have its home in the institution employing it—the hospital, orphan house, or whatever it is, being its proper abode and training-place. The initiation of these Societies is facilitated by thus doing away with the necessity and difficulty of provid-

ing special houses. Obviously any institution expecting to be so worked, must appropriate suitable accommodations for the workers.

2. No amount of funds is requisite for such a society. The Sisters would have their board, lodging and washing under the roof of the charity they serve (but of whose pecuniary affairs they had best have no management), and, as a rule, they would look for nothing beside. In this way is removed another point sometimes presented as an obstacle.

3. Each Sister would ordinarily have enough means of her own, or through private friends, for her few personal expenses. It is desirable such should be the case for other than pecuniary reasons. But sometimes there would be valuable candidates for admission, who could not provide for themselves. To meet this contingency, the institution using the Sisterhood might make it a part of its regular expenses to place statedly in the hands of an appointed treasurer a small sum toward a Sister's Fund, out of which to supply this or any other accidental demand of the association: or the Sisters might form such a fund among themselves. The fact that any

Sister is so aided should be known only to the Superintending Sister and the holder of the fund.

4. The Elder, or Superintending Sister would be the natural counsellor of the community. She directs the employment of the others, and is invested with enough control to secure efficient service, and to prevent any sudden rupture and lapses in the work. She would also attend, on behalf of the community, to any business transactions that might become necessary with the authorities of the institution they are engaegd in.

5. The few rules of the society would have regard to the allotment of work: the hours of rest, devotion, and recreation: becoming plainness of food and attire, and other domiciliary matters. They should be subscribed to by each associate on her admission to full membership, and she should hold herself bound by them as long as she continues in the community.

6. The prescribed term of service is three years, and this should be preceded by a probation, varying with circumstances, but never less than six months in duration; and the candidate should be ordinarily not under twenty-one years

of age, and not over forty. A short trial visit might with advantage be made a preliminary of this probation. A candidate could be received as a probationer on the judgment of the superintending Sister alone, but the vote of all the others should be necessary for admission to full membership. This prospect of a termination of their engagement, after three years, would go far with some to soothe any discontent or weariness that might steal over them; and, in the same light, the petty grievances which will sometimes start up in the happiest Community, instead of being magnified into seeds of disaffection, would pass for the trifles they are.

7. At the end of three years a Sister, if she desire, might renew her term of service, supposing that, as at first, she is accepted by the vote of the rest of the Community, and it is to this provision that we must look for a deepening and widening of the work, and for a succession of well-qualified heads for other similar institutions. Frequently when her engagement expired, the Sister would return to her own home; but sometimes, perhaps often, there would appear one of more tenacity of purpose, or of stronger faith

and love, not willing to live as she had done before joining the Association; and feeling constrained to work on after the same manner. Such a one might, as we have seen, renew her term of service where she is, or she might carry out her wishes, and, at the same time, have the refreshment and benefit of a change of work, by joining some other Sisterhood differently occupied, for a term of service: or if possessing administrative talent, and otherwise fit for headship, she might go forth and inaugurate a new Society, which, in its turn, would send out, now and again, new centres for other organizations, and so might such Associations be both multiplied and reproduced.

8th. Supposing there should be several of these Associations, engaged in so many different parishes or institutions; they would be independent of each other. There would be sisterly intercourse, perhaps kindly interchange of service, but no corporate relation would exist between them. This is necessary in the improbability of any central organization.

9. There should be a prescribed dress—not the affectation of some foreign religious habit, but

an adaptation (peculiar only in its plainness and simplicity), of the ordinary attire of a gentlewoman.

There are several common-sense reasons why the members of a Christian Sisterhood should dress alike.

1st. It promotes sisterly equality, precluding, like a clergyman's surplice, invidious differences of appearance between the more wealthy and the less well-provided members.

2d. It excludes eccentricities and unsuitablenesses.

3d. It is economical as to the outlay both of money and time.

4th. It is a badge of sisterly union, and as such is of value to the Community in much the same way as a soldier's uniform is to the regiment, or a scholar's gown and cap to the university.

Question 4. Can Associate, or Non-resident Sisters, be made an effective agency in connection with Sisterhoods?

Answer. In the Sisterhood of the Holy Communion provision was at one time made for the admission (of course as a subordinate arm of the service) of Associate or non-resident Sisters, who gave a certain number of hours a day and then returned to their homes. The experiment was fully tried, and after a few years was laid aside as a failure. It proved as unsatisfactory to the Associate as to her companions. Her heart seeking to be in two places was at rest in neither, and sometimes heart and conscience would stand at issue; so that, more than once has such a one said, in speaking of her embarrassments, "It would be easier for me to be a United Sister." Doubtless it would, for in this sense also it is true that we cannot serve two masters. A woman's heart is not formed to entertain, at the same time, two engrossing objects of interest; either her work must be first or society first; and if she tries to have it otherwise, she will often find herself painfully divided between the opposing claims. In a work there must be sacrifice. That which costs nothing is worth nothing; and if a woman would be a true, whole-hearted worker for the Lord, in the way we are supposing, she must separate herself, at least for the period of her engagement, from many things both dear and delightful. Nor shall she be without her reward in so doing, the reward of a freedom of mind and peace of soul which will shed over all her paths rays of a heavenly sunshine.

Question 5. Must there, then, be an entire withdrawal from all social ties?

Answer. No—only such a regulation of our intercourse with relatives and friends as shall make it the refreshment, not the governing business of the day. Indeed, proper provision for such intercourse as a recreation, and for regular out-door exercise, should be made in all these associations.

PRINCIPLES AND RULES

OF THE

SISTERHOOD OF THE HOLY COMMUNION.

I. FROM THE PRINCIPLES OF ASSOCIATION.

THE members of the Community are of two classes, United Sisters and Probationers.

The United Sisters are those who, after a satisfactory probation, are elected full members of the society.

The Probationary Sisters are those under

training for full membership, and are not ordinarily under twenty-one nor over forty years of age.

The vote of the United Sisters is necessary to full membership.

The probationary term is never less than six months, and may be prolonged at discretion.

The services of the Sisters are gratuitous, but they have their board and lodging free of expense.

The term of engagement for a United Sister is three years, renewable, if desired, at the expiration of the same, by the vote of the other Sisters, as at first.

The government of the Community devolves upon one of the United Sisters, known as the First Sister, to whom the others are expected to yield a cheerful obedience in all things pertaining to the ordering of the Community, and the work given it to do.

II. FROM THE RULES.

The Sisters are required to conform exactly to the appointed order of the day.

They dress alike, and as plainly and inexpensively as possible.

The visits of relatives and friends can be received by the Sisters only in their hours of recreation. No visits are expected on Sundays.

The Sisters have daily an allotted time for recreation, and during the summer months a vacation each of four weeks.

The First Sister has the discretionary power of dispensing with the observance of the rules. She directs the employment of the Sisters, both United and Probationary, in the hours allotted, and exercises a mother's care as to their health and comfort.

The Probationary Sister is expected to perform cheerfully the work given her to do, and, in a docile spirit, to receive the direction of any Sister under whose instruction she may be placed.

III. Questions for Self-Examination.

Selected and slightly altered from a series prepared by Pastor Fleidner, *with especial reference to Deaconesses employed in Hospitals.*

Concerning the Morning.

1. Have I, on waking, thought first of God, and lifted up my heart to Him in praise and thanksgiving?

2. Have I prayed for renewed grace and forgiveness, for fresh love, humility, and wisdom to enable me to do my duty for our Saviour Christ's sake?

3. Have I omitted to mention in my prayers those committed to my care, the Sisters, all who dwell with me, my relations, my spiritual pastor, and others whom I am bound so to remember?

4. Do I ask that I may, all the day, do every thing as in God's sight, seeking the approbation of my Saviour, and not to please men?

5. Do I rise punctually, and dress quickly, with due regard to propriety and neatness, but without ministering to vanity?

6. Do I in silence collect my thoughts and prepare for the united morning devotions? Have I been unnecessarily absent from these? Do I join in them with my whole heart, and seek to make them profitable to myself?

Concerning external Duties.

7. Do I take care that the ward of which I have charge is aired and arranged at the proper time?

8. Have I listened attentively to the direction of the physician, and observed punctually his

orders as to medicine, diet, etc., using no remedies not prescribed or sanctioned by him?

9. Am I careful to inform him of the patient's state, and, when necessary, of the particular effect of the medicines administered?

10. In attending to the bodily wants of the sick, have I done so kindly and faithfully? Do I see that their clothing, diet, etc., are sufficient and of the right kind; and when this is not the case, do I at once give information to the superintending Sister?

11. Have I been prudent and careful in using the various provisions and appliances of the Hospital, remembering that the institution is supported by charity?

12. Have I performed my duty without noise or display? Have I been obliging, patient, cheerful, and watchful, as becomes one who serves the sick for the Lord's sake?

13. Have I been just and equal in my treatment of the patients, ministering to them without partiality?

Concerning Spiritual Duties to the Sick.

14. In reading and talking to the sick, have I

tried to point them to the love of God in chastising them (Heb. xii. 5-12); showing them that He allows us to suffer in the flesh that we may cease from sin (1 Pet. iv. 1); that He makes whole that we may sin no more (John v. 14); that the works of God may be made manifest in us (John ix. 1-3); that God may be glorified thereby? (John xi. 4.)

15. Have I procured for my patients a sufficiency of spiritual food—*e. g.*, of religious books, and above all, the Bible, and have I tried to direct them so that they might read profitably?

16. Have I sought diligently to cheer and help them by talking, reading, and praying with them, as opportunity offered?

17. Have I named to the clergyman any especially needing his assistance, and, when he desired it, informed him of the state of their minds?

18. Have I considered my patients as placed in Christ's school, and, when necessary, warned and exhorted them to listen to God's call to repentance?

19. Have I striven to promote in them resignation to God's will, teaching them to cast all their anxieties upon Him?

20. Have I checked too much talk about worldly things, especially arguments on politics and public affairs?

21. Have I been careful by no means to dispute with the sick about religion, nor to allow them to dispute with one another?

22. Have I endeavored to cultivate mutual kindness and good will between the different sick ones entrusted to me?

23. If engaged with the sick children, have I tried to train their hearts and souls aright, nourishing and cherishing them as the lambs of Christ's flock?

Concerning my Conduct to the Sisters, to the Superiors of the House, and Others.

24. Have I endeavored to show sincere love to those living with me, especially to the Sisters, that we may be of one mind in the Lord? In any dispute that has arisen, have I allowed "the sun to go down upon my wrath," or sought Christian reconciliation before going to rest?

25. Have I always been obedient to the Sisters immediately set over me, as well as to the other superiors of the house, with child-like submission,

without murmuring, according to the admonition of St. Paul? (Phil. ii. 14.) Have I allowed any feelings of bitterness, or anger, or dislike, to arise in my mind toward those who have blamed me? Or, if such arose, did I quickly recognize their sinfulness, and strive to overcome them by confessing them to the Lord, and beseeching Him to give me a kind and affectionate heart?

26. If any of the duties imposed upon me seemed too difficult or unsuited to me, did I mention this privately to the superintending Sister, or did I complain to the others, and judge her uncharitably?

27. Have I concealed from the superiors of the institution anything which conscientiously, or by the rules of the house, I was bound immediately to tell them, whether it related to myself, to others, or to the hospital?

28. If other Sisters have been placed with me that I might direct them or receive assistance from them, have I always treated them with kindness, meekness, and humility, as our Saviour teaches us by His example (John xiii. 2-15), and by His word? (Mark x. 42-45; Matt. xii. 50.) If it has been my duty to find fault or reprove,

have I done so in a spirit of holy love, as privately and kindly as possible, both in words and manner?

29. Has the fear of man, or the desire to please man, kept me silent when I ought to have rebuked or admonished?

30. In my work have I looked upon my own things instead of on those of others? Have I sought to lay the difficult and disagreeable duties upon others instead of doing them, when I could, myself, as a servant of the Sisters, for Jesus' sake?

31. Have I kept my tongue in check, eschewing all frivolous and useless gossiping, both with the Sisters, patients, doctors, and all others residing in the house, and avoiding an unsuitable intimacy with the two last classes of persons?

32. Have I shown a partial love toward some Sisters, and, on the contrary, repelled others?

33. Have I, during the time of my service in this part of the Lord's vineyard, endeavored always to maintain a serious, dignified, and reserved behavior, becoming a Deaconess of the Lord?

Concerning the Training of my own Soul, and my Improvement in the Duties of my Office.

34. Do I accustom myself daily to hold communion with the Lord at other times besides the fixed hours of prayer?

35. Do I diligently read the Holy Scriptures, that they may be profitable to me for doctrine, for reproof, for correction, for instruction in righteousness?

36. Have I been led to acknowledge my sinfulness by the remembrance of the Redeemer crucified for me, and do I earnestly pray for forgiveness through Him?

37. Do I endeavor to prove myself a disciple of the Lord Jesus by a constant endeavor to become lowly in my own eyes, by firmly renouncing the world and its pleasures, by purifying myself from all pollution of the flesh and the spirit, and especially from my besetting sins, by a daily advancing in holiness and the fear of God, and by bringing forth the fruits of the Spirit?

38. Have I diligently thought on my baptismal vows, and on their renewal in Confirmation and Holy Communion? Have I embraced the

opportunities I have had of receiving the Holy Communion, preparing myself for it by diligent prayer and self-examination, and by meditation upon the love of Christ?

39. Do I try to enrich my mind with Christian knowledge, and other information useful and profitable for my office? Do I take advantage of all the means of improvement open to me in the different departments of Sisters' work?

40. Have I taken proper care of my bodily health by exercise in the open air at the appointed times, and by observing the rules as to meals and rest?

41. Have I sought to be faithful in that which is least, obeying all the prescribed rules, for the Lord's sake, however unimportant they may seem, that no loss or injury may occur to the Sisterhood through my fault?

42. Have I at all times, whether actively employed in the duties of my office or not, behaved as the Lord's servant, giving offence to none, but rather seeking to please all for their good.

43. When not permitted to see the fruits of my labor, have I grown desponding and listless in my work, instead of hoping even against hope,

and remembering that the sower must wait patiently for the blessing that gives the increase?

44. When allowed to see the good seed spring up in the hearts of any among whom I labor, do I give all to the glory of God, acknowledging myself an unprofitable servant?

45. Do I daily endeavor to give up my will entirely to God, "forgetting those things which are behind," even all my once favorite thoughts and wishes, that they may not disturb me in my chosen service, nor hinder me in pressing forward to the prize of our high calling in Christ Jesus?

46. Is it my desire to be dead indeed unto the world, and to walk by faith, having my life hid with Christ in God?

47. Am I conscious that my aim in thought and deed is to advance the glory of God in the salvation of men?

SISTERS' HYMN.

Together let us bless the Lord,
   Together magnify His name,
Who moves our hearts with sweet accord,
   Union in His dear cross to claim.

Sisters in Christ! All-holy tie,
   Fruit of His own electing love,
The fellowship and lineage high
   Of sainted companies above.

Workers with Christ! All-holy toil,
   Easy, through Him, when most severe;
Cares shall not daunt, nor sin shall soil,
   So that we always feel Him near.

Earth shall not lure. No! Saviour-God,
   Our steps shall on Thy will attend;
Gladly we go where Thou hast trod—
   Thy glory all our aim and end.

Thou all our portion and delight,
   Thy love the brightness of our days;
We, faint and feeble, Thou our might,
   Our weakness turning to Thy praise.

Yea, we will praise with all Heaven's host,
   Together magnify again,
Thee, Father, Son, and Holy Ghost,
   God, our own God, Amen, Amen.

PRAYER FOR UNION WITH CHRIST.

O Lord Jesus Christ, who art the true Vine, and Thy disciples the branches, grant, if I be indeed a living branch, that I may bring forth more fruit! I mourn before Thee my past unfruitfulness, my selfish ease, my compliances with the world, my divided affections, the unreality of my life, as one professing to be united to Thee. O, renew me with the quickening power of Thy Spirit; revive me with Thy grace; give me henceforth to abide in Thee; gather up my thoughts, my purposes, my desires unto Thyself. Let me have no aim out of Thee. Enable me so to order my life as shall best help me to union and communion with Thee. Let me, in very deed, take up my cross daily and follow Thee—Thee, my Lord and my God, my meek and lowly Master, my suffering Redeemer, who didst not please Thyself, but wentest about doing good. Let me never more live unto myself. Let Thy love within me show forth itself in love to all around me, to all whom Thou hast vouchsafed to call Thy brethren. As Thou hast prayed for us that we may be one, even as Thou and the

Father art one, grant us to know something of this divine fellowship. Thou hast bidden us to love one another, even as thou hast loved us. Lord, kindle then in us some beginnings of this love that passeth knowledge. Lord, teach us and we shall learn. Lord, draw us to Thy cross by the cords of Thy love, reaching unto Thy throne in glory. Hearken, for Thine own mercies' sake, O blessed Saviour, who art with the Father and the Holy Ghost, one God, world without end. *Amen.*

2.
Order of Deaconesses of the Diocese of Maryland.

THE Order of Deaconesses of the Diocese of Maryland originated in St. Andrew's Parish, Baltimore, under the ministry of the Rev. Horace Stringfellow. In 1855, two ladies gave themselves to the work of ministering to the poor, and became residents of St. Andrew's Rectory for that purpose. With the sanction and approval of the Bishop of the Diocese, a house was secured and opened, under the name of St. Andrew's Infirmary, and the number of those connected with the work speedily increased to four resident and four associate Sisters, whose aims and work may be gathered from the following extract from an early Report of the Infirmary:

"The Deaconesses look to no organization of persons to furnish the pecuniary aid required by the demands of their position........... Their first efforts have been for the destitute sick. Out of the house, they minister daily to the suffering and destitute sick, wherever found, some only requiring temporary medical aid and nursing; others, whom God has chastened with more continuous suffering, requiring, in their penury and desolation, constant care and continual ministration."

After the sick, their cares are given to a school set up for vagrant children.

Besides the Charity School, they carry on a Church School for training such children of the more favored classes as may be committed to them.

The following are the Forms for setting apart Deaconesses, for Devotion, for Annual Meetings, Rules of Discipline, &c.; of the Deaconesses of the Diocese of Maryland:

FORM OF SETTING APART THOSE TO BE ADMITTED TO THE ORDER OF DEACONESS, OR AS PROBATIONERS.

Dearly beloved in the Lord, we are met together in the fear of God, and trusting in His Holy Name to receive and ratify the pledge of obedient and loving service offered by these our Sisters, whom, on the recommendation of those entrusted with their care and government, the whole body of the Deaconesses has by an unanimous voice admitted to its fellowship: and at the same time to admit to the commencement of due and prescribed probation, others, our Sisters, whose hearts, as we trust, the Lord has moved with a desire to serve Him in this ministration, and whom we find, on due inquiry, to be apt and meet for such probationary admission; and furthermore, to recognize formally and solemnly, by one joint act, as an associate in the work another Sister, for whom, in the Providence of God, a post of immediate duty offers, not admitting at present of her entrance on the customary probationary course.

In their several places and degrees, these our Sisters desire to serve their Heavenly Lord and Master Jesus Christ in the persons of His poor and weak and suffering members. For His sake they seek the privilege of living only to serve the widow and the orphan, the sick and the destitute, the wretched and distressed. Under His blessing, through the constituted authority of His

Church, they desire to follow those holy women who of old ministered to the Lord in person, and those whom His apostles admitted to be helpers in the work, and succorers of themselves and others.

In such following of the holy examples of the days of old, these our Sisters are presented to be received and sanctioned in their several degrees. They are of good report, as was required of those first admitted to serve tables in the Church. They have been diligent in prayer for the Holy Spirit and the wisdom from above. They hold, as we are persuaded, the mystery of the faith in a pure conscience, and we humbly trust, that taught of God to know their own impurity, they have turned with a repentance not to be repented of to the Saviour of sinners, and have heard of Him the small still voice which reveals the peace that passeth understanding and purifies the heart by faith. In outward walk and conversation they have been proved by periods of probation varying in length, but in all abundantly sufficing for the satisfaction of those with whom the responsibility of judgment on their fitness lies. Their skilfulness and unblameableness in the service of the sick and poor have been duly tested, their docility and orderly obedience to the superior and the physician in their several kinds of ministration have been tried, and under the care and direction of their spiritual pastor they have learned to watch and supply the spiritual wants of those under their care as far as is consistent with their office and station in the Church. To body and mind, in solacing and comforting by day and by night, they have been taught, and have been diligent in laboring to minister relief for the afflicted and the miserable, "diligently following every good work."

Thus approved, and found worthy to fulfil the duties of Deaconess, our......sisters here present *are* this day to be admitted thereunto, under the invocation of the Blessed Name of Him whom they desire to serve.

But it is fitting, dear Sisters, that here, in the presence of God and this congregation, the duties to which you are about to devote yourselves should be again laid before you.

You are to be servants of the Church of God, as Deaconesses, specially in ministering to the sick and poor, but also, if need be, to prisoners and outcasts, to the destitute and oppressed, to helpless and orphan children, and to the abject and friendless penitent. To some or all of these it will be your duty, according as you shall be specially directed, to render service in a threefold capacity: as,

(1.) Servants of the Lord Jesus.

(2.) Servants of the sick and poor and needy of every class, for Jesus' sake.

(3.) Servants in the Lord to one another.

First, as servants of the Lord Jesus, you are not only bound, as any Christian, to live to the honor of God, but you have also taken it to be the special object of your life to serve Him with all your powers in the weak and suffering members of His Body. You are therefore so much the more bound to die to all the pleasures, honors, riches and joys of the world; to seek your joy in this service of love, through gratitude to Him who took upon Him the form of a servant, and suffered for you even unto death, the death upon the cross. In this service you are neither to seek for nor expect any abundance of earthly reward; having food and raiment, you are to be therewith content.

You are not to seek honor nor praise from man. You must be willing and glad, if need so be, to go forth unto Jesus, bearing the reproach. You cannot seek earthly pleasure and ease.. You have set out to deny yourselves, take up your cross daily, and follow on, bearing it for Him whom your souls have learned to love.

What privilege, what honor, shall you thus enjoy! You are to minister to Him whom it is the highest reward and honor of the holy angels to rejoice in serving, the King of kings and Lord of lords—to serve Him as His handmaidens, to wait in closest attendance upon Him in His members.

As Mary of Bethany had always before her eyes the one thing needful, and therefore rejoiced to sit at Jesus' feet, but was also ready, when it was permitted her, to wait upon and to anoint Him, even for His burying—as she did not shrink from her work of love, from expense, from trouble, or from the derision of men, so must you always desire, on the one hand, to hear the Lord Jesus in His Word and ministry, on the other to serve Him in His members with a love which beareth all things, believeth all things, hopeth all things, endureth all things. Then will His glorious promise be yours. He will say to you, "I was naked, and ye clothed Me; I was sick, and ye visited Me; I was in prison, and ye came unto Me." "Whoso receiveth a little child in My Name, receiveth Me." "Come ye blessed of my Father, inherit the kingdom prepared for you from the foundation of the world."

Secondly, as servants of the sick and needy, for Jesus' sake. As you serve the Lord in them, so are you to serve them as He would have you, and after the example left you by His servants. St. Paul made himself a servant to all, that he might gain the more. So must you, in serving those to whom you minister, seek to win, not their praise, not the good report of men, not their love and gratitude, for its own sake, but themselves, for gain unto Christ your Lord. His work in saving souls must be your end and aim, love and submission to Him, the Saviour of your souls, your ruling motive.

Your service, therefore, must be rendered not in such weak indulgence as might strengthen waywardness of inclination or perversity of will, but always with the holy seal of parental affection, as to those for whom you must give an account, whose souls you are the Lord's agents to recover for himself.

Thirdly, as servants one to another, it will be your duty, my sisters, when working together in your several degrees and stations, to show in every way that love which leads us in lowliness of mind to esteem others better than ourselves. Whosoever will be great among you, let her be the servant of all. If you are one by a living faith in our common Lord and Saviour, a tie nearer and stronger than the closest ties of blood binds you together in spirit and affection. You live together and work together as the acknowledged daughters of Him who has said, "By this shall all men know that ye are my disciples, if ye love one another;" and who at the same time taught us, as He humbled Himself, to show His love unto His own, by doing them menial service of the lowliest kind, to follow His example in gladly humbling ourselves in offices of love the one toward the other.

In such loving lowliness, dear Sisters, your service to Christ is to be discharged, with childlike obedience and respect to the superiors in your association and spiritual pastors, who are over you in the Lord, and labor among you in parental love.

In the presence of God and of this congregation, I now demand of you, Are you ready and determined faithfully to fulfil the office of a Deaconess, as it has been now set forth, and to keep the Rules under which you are associated as such, in the fear of the Lord, according to His holy word?

Answer. I am ready, and am so determined.

Bishop. May our Lord Jesus Christ, the Chief Shepherd and Bishop of your souls, accept and seal your profession and promise as yea and Amen in Him, and own you as His, and with His blessing crown you forever. *Amen.*

¶ *Then the Sisters are received, all kneeling.*

God the Father, God the Son, God the Holy Ghost bless you in your purpose and work, make you faithful unto death, and give you the crown of everlasting life. *Amen.*

¶ *Then the Deaconesses rising:*

Draw near and give to me and to the First

Deaconess your right hands, in confirmation of your promise and token of your fellowship.

¶ *The Deaconesses, received successively advance, and each takes the right hand, first of the Bishop, and then of the First Deaconess, with her right hand.*
¶ *Then all again kneeling.*

Bishop. Let us who are here assembled and desire for these Deaconesses salvation and blessing, pray for them.

The Lord be with you.

Ans. And with thy spirit.

Bishop. O Lord, show thy mercy upon us.

Ans. And grant us Thy salvation.

Bishop. O God, make clean our hearts within us.

Ans. And take not Thy Holy Spirit from us.

PRAYER.

O Father of mercy, who hast led these Thy servants to Thy Son, so that they have given themselves up to Him for His own peculiar possession, and desire to serve Him with all their powers of body and soul, in administering to the sick, and poor, and ignorant, and destitute, we humbly beseech Thee be merciful unto them, and direct their hearts into Thy love and into the patient waiting for Christ, that in Thy household the Church, nourished and strengthened by Thy word and ordinances, they may live and work in Thee, and rejoice in Thy favor always, through Jesus Christ our Lord. *Amen.*

O Lord Jesus Christ, Thou merciful High-Priest, who hast purchased these souls with Thy most precious Blood, Thine they are, bought of Thee and joined to Thee in Thy holy covenant. They have over and above devoted themselves to Thine especial service. Graciously accept the gift, poor and unworthy as they acknowledge it to be. Enlighten them with the bright beams of Thy truth, strengthen their weakness by Thy power, comfort and support them by Thy continual presence, and give them of Thine own meek and lowly spirit ; that acknowledging themselves to be unprofitable servants before Thee, they may, in singleness of heart, desire to be and do nothing of themselves, but only to the honor of Thy glorious name, now and for evermore. *Amen.*

O God the Holy Ghost, Thou Spirit of peace and comfort, replenish these members of Thy household with Thy peace, that they, as Thy messengers and instruments, may bring peace and consolation to the homes and families of the sick and miserable, and in their companionship to their associates in the work ; and grant that they may ever be adorned with the ornament of a meek and quiet spirit, and so govern themselves in cheerful obedience toward their superiors, that in performing their commands they may, with a glad mind and will, render obedience unto Thee ; all which we ask through the prevailing merits of our Lord and Saviour Jesus Christ, to whom with Thee, O Father, and Thee, O Holy Ghost, be all honor and glory, world without end. *Amen.*

HYMN 179.

¶ *Then the Offertory, &c. in the administration of the Holy Communion are proceeded with.*

¶ *And the Deaconesses, Probationers and Associate Sisters partake, each degree severally in its order.*

¶ *If there are Probationers to be admitted; or Associates to be received and recognized, the Admission or Reception shall take place; or if both, each in its order, as here named, immediately after the prayer for the newly received Deaconess, and before the Offertory.*

¶ *The Deaconesses having retired from the altar-rail, the First Deaconess shall bring up thither the persons to be admitted Probationers or Associates, or if there be both, each in their order, the Associates after the Probationers shall have retired, and shall present them to the Bishop.*

Bishop. Dear Sisters in Christ, in behalf of the United Deaconesses of Maryland, it is my duty now to inform you of your admission to be Probationers for the office of Deaconess, on recommendation of the Rector and First Deaconess. You have heard the charge given to the Sisters just received, and the promise made by them, and have joined in the prayers made in their behalf. Before you, that charge set forth the character and work toward which your aim and efforts are to be henceforth steadily directed. That promise embodied the pledge implied in your assumption of the probationary relation. Those prayers, in spirit and in substance, must become the unceasing petition of your soul, in behalf of yourselves, that you may attain to that good degree to which you have been admitted to look forward, and in behalf of those with whom you are now associated, that they with you, and you with them, may be sharers in a common blessing, through the mercy of your Father, the grace of Jesus Christ our Lord, and the comfort and strengthening of the Holy Ghost. You are to continue Probationers during the times respectively prescribed by the Rector and Chief Deaconess, and until a vote of the United Deaconesses agreeing to your reception. Until then, be it your daily endeavor to grow in grace and in humility, docility, meekness, and faithful diligence, to labor after the acquirement of thorough fitness for the department of work to which you shall be assigned : in which may God our Father, and the Lord Jesus Christ, with the comfort and help of the Holy Ghost, bless, preserve, and prosper you. *Amen.*

¶ *The Probationers having retired, the First Deaconess shall bring forward and present the person (s) to be received as (an) Associate (s).*

Bishop. Beloved in the Lord, on recommendation of the First Deaconess, with the approval of the Rector, you have been received by vote of the United Deaconesses to be [a *resident* or a *detached*] Associate, in the manner and for the purposes agreed on between you and the First Deaconess. In pursuance of that agreement, you are faithfully to observe the rules of the Deaconnesses relating to associates in their work, and to observe the directions which, in accordance with those rules and your agreement, may from time to time be given. The charge which in your hearing has been given to your Sisters now received as Deaconesses, is equally your lesson for your guidance in the fellowship with them to which you are admitted. The promise which they have made pertains to you also, in the degree of your association. Is it your mind and will, in oneness of spirit with them, in like faith and hope for the love of the same Lord, to strive together in your degree and lot to do Him humble and cheerful service?

¶ *They shall all severally answer,*

Yes.

Bishop. May God, who hath given you that heart and will, evermore bless you in a faithful performance of the same, through Jesus Christ our Lord. *Amen.*

HYMN 179.

¶ *Then the Offertory, &c., in the administration of the Holy Communion, are proceeded with.*

¶ *After the Gloria in Excelsis, the received Deaconesses and Probationers and Associates, if any, shall draw near to the altar-rail, and standing in order before it, shall be thus addressed:*

Bishop. Ye have now, beloved in the Lord (in your several degrees), entered upon the especial privilege of service unto Christ in His vineyard;

to you has been especially entrusted the high honor of ministering to your Saviour in His weak and suffering members. Arise then, arise, my Sisters, and gird yourselves, as the wise Virgins, for His service. Behold the Bridegroom cometh, go ye out to meet Him with loins girded and burning lights. He standeth at the door and knocketh, in form indeed of a servant, in the needy and destitute to whom your cares and ministrations are to be given. Open then unto Him, that He may come in and sup. Feed Him in the hungry, clothe Him in the naked, receive Him in His little ones, visit Him in the friendless and destitute, the prisoner and the oppressed; bind up his wounds and render nursing care to His infirmities in the sick, and make Him ready for the burial in the dead, whom for His sake you prepare for their last resting-place.

In such discharge of your blessed office, hardships and difficulties are to be looked for. The heart may become faint and the head confused, the hands hang down with weariness, and the feeble knees refuse to do their office. But then, too, the heavenly Bridegroom will be with you as the Lord of glory. He has given you, in the spiritual food which you have been even now receiving, the assurance of His Presence to support and strengthen, to assist and abundantly to reward all such good works as He has prepared for you to walk in. In Him be strong. In Him be glad with holy boldness. In His might and consolation go forth, ready and able to do or suffer whatsoever in His loving wisdom He shall see fit to set before you in your work for Him.

¶ *Let us pray.*

Almighty and everlasting God, who dost vouchsafe to accept and bless the humble service of those to whom, in Thy great goodness, Thou hast given a willing heart, grant, we beseech Thee, to these Thy handmaidens, such willingness of heart, such humble quietness of spirit and confidence in Thee, such sincerity and godly simplicity in the denial of self and glad endurance of privation, hardship, thanklessness and reproach in the service of Thy poor and the little ones of Thy flock, and such faithful perseverance in meekness, lowliness, and long-suffering, and abounding charity among each other, and towards all men, as may obtain Thy merciful acceptance and overflowing blessing for their work, through the alone merits and intercession of Jesus Christ, Thy Son our Lord. *Amen.*

¶ *Then shall follow the Benediction.*

First Prayer for Chapter Meetings.

Almighty and most merciful Father, who by thy Son our Lord Jesus Christ, in the day of his visible dwelling among men, didst accept the ministrations of women to His sacred person, vouchsafe to regard our supplications in behalf of these Thine handmaids now assembled, in the desire and endeavor, in the devotion of themselves and of their services, to prove their love to Thee. Accept and bless the purpose of their hearts, in so far as it is Thy work, the fruit of Thy word and Holy Spirit. Thou who knowest the hearts of all, search and try the ground of the hearts of Thy servants; see whether there be in them a spirit of entire devotion to Thy service, and create it, if there be not, and strengthen it if there be. Overcome in them, O Lord, the dullness and slowness of their minds, and make them to understand more and more of the unsearchable riches of Thy grace. Overcome the earthliness of their affections; make them to love Thee as well as they can love at all, and suffer them to have no affection independent of Thee. Overcome in us all, especially, O God our Saviour, our self-love; root it out of our hearts, as Thy grace only can, and implant in its stead love to Thee as the great motive of our life, the spring of all our thoughts, and words, and actions.

Thou hast left us, O Lord, the poor and miserable; saying, Inasmuch as ye did it unto one of the least of these, ye did it unto me; and grant to these Thy servants grace and opportunity to spend their days in ministering to such in Thy Name. Touch all our hearts with heavenly pity. Fill all our souls with holy zeal. Increase our faith. Root and ground us in love. Clothe us with humility. Make for each and all of us our way plain before us, and give us strength and courage patiently to surmount every obstacle with which Thou mayest see fit to try us. Breathe upon Thy whole Church the spirit of love unfeigned. Give us for darkness light; for prejudice the charity that hopeth all things; for strife and envyings, a holy emulation in Thy service, and for Thy glory.

All this we ask, O heavenly Father, for Thine

own mercies' sake, and for the sake of the infinite merits of Thy true and only Son; to whom, with Thee and the Holy Spirit, one God over all, blessed forever, be honor, praise and glory, now and evermore. *Amen.*

RULES FOR THE ORDER OF DEACONESSES OF THE DIOCESE OF MARYLAND.

1. This organization of Christian women, under the pastoral care of the Bishop of the Diocese, is established for the management of an Infirmary, the formation of Church Schools, and such other works of charity as may be deemed expedient.

2. The members of this Society are divided into three classes. (1) The United Deaconesses. (2) Probationers. (3) The Associate Deaconesses.

3. The United Deaconesses are those who, having passed through their Probationary terms, and contemplating a permanent continuance in the Order, are admitted, upon application to the Bishop, by an unanimous election of the United Deaconesses. They must be at least twenty years of age.

They reside in the Parental House, unless being called by Providence to some other sphere of duty, they depart with the full sanction of the Bishop and the Order, still however retaining their allegiance to the Society, continuing always subject to its rule, statedly rendering a report of their work, to the First Deaconess, and holding themselves in readiness to be recalled whenever deemed necessary or proper by those in authority.

All the United Deaconesses are bound to hold themselves in readiness to be sent by the Bishop to any other field, whenever it is deemed necessary for the promotion of the object of the organization.

4. The government and regulation of the Society is vested in the First Deaconess, who is nominated to the office by the Bishop, and unanimously elected by the United Deaconesses, and to whom all the other members shall render cheerful obedience. She shall have charge of all money given to the Society, which being first dedicated to Almighty God, through the Offertory, shall by her be dispensed as she in her discretion shall deem best for the support of the

members and for the furtherance of the objects for which the Society is organized. She shall keep accurate accounts of all income and outlay, and exhibit the same to the Bishop of the Diocese as often as may be required, and to the United Deaconesses once every month.

5. The United Deaconesses shall assume an economical habit, conforming in expense, style, and color, which shall be black or gray, as the necessity of their position may require.

6. Each lady shall be furnished with the sum of $100 per annum for her personal expenses and private charities, while in active service, and during sickness and old age she is in all things provided for at the expense of the organization.

7. Every United Deaconess is forbidden to receive fee or compensation for her services, but whenever remuneration is made, it must be paid to the organization, and placed in a Reserve Fund to provide for the wants of aged, infirm or sick Deaconesses.

8. A Deaconess is at liberty to retire from the Association six months after having addressed her resignation to the Bishop of the Diocese, which term he may shorten if desirable. He

also has the right to dismiss any Deaconess when, for improper conduct, or for any other grave consideration, he may deem the measure necessary.

9. It shall be the part of the First Deaconess daily to assign an outline of duty to each member of the Order, beginning the day with prayer for the Divine aid in the discharge of their several duties.

10. Six hours of Prayer—6 and 9 A. M., 12, 3, 6 and 9 P. M., shall be observed by the United Deaconesses, wherever they may be, or whatever may be their employments—those who are sufficiently disengaged assembling in the Chapel or Private Oratory for such services as are appointed, and those who are ministering or employed elsewhere using mentally an established form for the set hours, and meditating on such topics for the day as may be pointed out by their spiritual Director. On Friday preceding the Holy Communion, at 3 P. M., the whole body, if possible, shall assemble with the Pastor in charge for his direction, counsel, and blessing.

11. The Feasts and Fasts of the Church shall be duly observed by such relaxation or by such

increased abstinence as the care of the sick, and the due performance of duty may permit.

All the members are entitled to an annual season of rest and freedom from care, according as their needs, their health, and the wants of the Institution shall determine.

Hours of visiting and receiving visits shall be so limited as not to interfere with the daily discharge of duty.

12. Probationers may be received for three months or longer, as shall be determined by the Bishop and the United Deaconesses on their entrance. They shall be placed under the charge of one of the United Deaconesses, in order to be fitted for the departments they are expected to occupy. During their probationary term they form part of the family, and in all things conform to its rules and regulations.

OF ASSOCIATES.

13. Any one wishing to become an Associate, must hand in her name to the First Deaconess, with the time she wishes to devote to the work. If approved by the whole body, she shall, as often as practicable, meet at the Noon Services

for the purpose of united Prayer, and for receiving directions for her daily work from the First Deaconess, to whom she is in all things to refer, as the head of the Organization, and to whom she shall render a full report once a month.

14. It shall be the aim of the whole Association to increase its operations by an increase of members, and by an extension of the various departments of works of charity, as contemplated in Article 1.

INTERIOR DISCIPLINE.

1. Each Deaconess has a distinct department, division or subdivision of work assigned her by the Chief Deaconess.

2. Once assigned such department, she shall be changed only with the consent of the Deaconess herself, or else with the advice and consent of a majority of the Deaconesses in Chapter assembled.

3. For the state and duties of such department, &c., the Deaconess in charge is responsible to the Chief Deaconess. Any complaint concerning it must be made directly to the Deaconess in charge; and only in case of alleged neglect of

such complaint by her, to be carried to the Chief Deaconess.

4. The Chief Deaconess may, and is bound to notice any neglect or deficiency in any department, &c., by direct communication with the Deaconess in charge.

5. No censure or reproof shall be addressed by the Chief Deaconess to any Deaconess or Probationer in the presence of any third person, but directions as to the discharge of duty or orders concerning duties to be performed are not under any circumstances to be understood to convey or imply censure or reproof.

6. Any Deaconess or Probationer shall have the right of appeal from censure or reproof by the Chief Deaconess to the Rector, or in his absence the Vice-Rector; but such appeal must be made at the first opportunity, with the least possible delay.

7. Gentleness in the conveyal of direction or reproof, and meekness in the reception, will be the study of all; and each shall in all humility help others to its observance.

8. No grievance or complaint of any Deaconess or Probationer against either the Chief or any

other Deaconess or Probationer shall be the subject of conversation between the aggrieved and any other, except the one occasioning it.

9. It is a general rule and agreement to be understood and observed by all, that neither by talking nor by listening shall conversation concerning misunderstandings or difficulties between members of the Sisterhood, or concerning grievances or complaints of any member be entered into or allowed.

FORM OF SERVICE TO BE USED AT A PUBLIC MEETING, OR ANNIVERSARY OF THE ORDER.

Sentences.

This is a faithful saying, and these things I will that thou affirm constantly, that they which have believed in God might be careful to maintain good works, for necessary uses, that they be not unfruitful.—*Titus* iii. 14.

Charge them that they do good; that they be rich in good works, ready to distribute, willing to communicate; laying up for themselves a good foundation against the time to come, that they may lay hold on eternal life.—1 *Tim.* vi. 17, 18.

The silver is Mine, and the gold is Mine, saith the Lord of Hosts.—*Haggai* ii. 8.

Not by might nor by power, but by my Spirit, saith the Lord of Hosts.—*Zechariah* iv. 6.

VERSICLES.

Our help is in the Name of the Lord.

Ans. Who hath made heaven and earth.

Blessed be the Name of the Lord.

Ans. Henceforth, world without end.

O Lord, open thou our lips.

Ans. And our mouth shall show forth Thy praise.

¶ *Then shall be said from the Psalter Psalm cxi. with the Gloria Patri, and Psalm cxlv. with the Gloria Patri.*

¶ *Then shall be read the Lesson, thus announced: The Lesson is written in the   chapter of*

¶ *After the Lesson shall be sung from the Psalms in metre, Selections 96th last 4 verses, and 69th, last 2 verses.*

Dominus vobiscum.

The Lord be with you.

Ans. And with thy spirit.

Minister. Let us pray.

O Lord, show Thy mercy upon us.

Ans. And grant us Thy salvation.

O God, make clean our hearts within us.

Ans. And take not Thy Holy Spirit from us.
Our Father, &c.

COLLECTS.

Almighty and everlasting God, who dost govern all things in heaven and earth ; Mercifully hear the supplications of Thy people, and grant us Thy peace all the days of our life ; through Jesus Christ our Lord. *Amen.*

O God, forasmuch as without Thee we are not able to please Thee ; Mercifully grant that Thy Holy Spirit may in all things direct and rule our hearts ; through Jesus Christ our Lord. *Amen.*

Lord, we beseech Thee to keep Thy household, the Church, in continual godliness ; that through Thy protection it may be free from all adversities, and devoutly given to serve Thee, in good works, to the glory of Thy Name ; through Jesus Christ our Lord. *Amen.*

Stir up, we beseech Thee, O Lord, the wills of Thy faithful people ; that they plenteously bringing forth the fruit of good works, may by Thee be plenteously rewarded ; through Jesus Christ our Lord. *Amen.*

THE PRAYER.

Almighty and everlasting God our Heavenly Father, who through Thy Son our Lord, hast called us to a house eternal in the heavens, vouchsafe, we beseech Thee, to prosper with Thy blessing the undertaking [in which Thy servants of this household are engaged of maintaining] [*we are now making ready*] for the needy and afflicted, the widow and the fatherless, the sick and destitute, a place of shelter and relief. O prosper Thou [*their*] [*our*] handiwork, and bring it to good effect. Make the hearts of Thy people ready to devise liberal things toward it, and strengthen Thou their hands to do a work acceptable unto Thee, through the prevailing merits and intercession of our only Mediator and Advocate, Jesus Christ Thy Son. *Amen.*

O Lord Jesus Christ, who hast called the needy and distressed Thy brethren, and hast graciously vouchsafed to regard what is done unto them in Thy name as done unto Thyself, look now in Thy great love upon us Thy servants, and upon this work in which we are gathered together in Thy Name, and so let Thy Holy Spirit fill and rule our hearts, that love for Thee, and for Thy poor in Thee, may make us to abound in ministrations of mercy, liberality, pitifulness and true compassion. Of such graces and their fruits in holy works, may this place [*be more and more*] [*become*] the honored home and centre, and its immates and conductors humble, but bright examples, shining as lights kindled from Thy light before all Thy spiritual household, to the glory of Thy grace; whom, with the Father and the Holy Ghost, we worship ever, one God, world without end. *Amen.*

O, Holy Ghost, Eternal God, Author and Giver of the wisdom from above, that is gentle, easy to be entreated, full of mercy and good fruits, shed forth, we beseech Thee, that wisdom in rich abundance, not only on all Thy servants who are or shall be banded together in Thy grace and strength for the conduct of this good work, in its several parts and ministries, but also on us now assembled under Thy guidance, and in trust in Thee that both they and we may be Thy blessed instruments of spreading Thy manifold gifts abroad, and kindling with fervent zeal the hearts of all those among whom we live and have our daily walk and conversation, that men may glorify our Father in heaven; whom with Jesus Christ His Son, and Thee, our Comforter and Sanctifier, we praise and bless, we worship and glorify, One only God, now and everlastingly, world without end. *Amen.*

¶ *2 Corinthians xiii. 14.*

The grace of our Lord, &c.

¶ *The Hymn,* 203, *last three verses.*
¶ *The Statement of the Trustees.*

ADDRESSES.

¶ *The Gloria in Excelsis.*
¶ *Collects. "Direct,"&c. "Almighty God, the fountain," &c.*

THE BLESSING.

A PRAYER FOR DEACONESSES, ASSOCIATES, AND OTHERS.

Almighty and everlasting God, who dost vouchsafe to accept and bless the humble service of those to whom, in Thy great goodness, Thou hast given a willing heart, grant, we beseech Thee, to these Thy handmaidens, such willingness of heart, such humble quietness of spirit, and confidence in Thee, such sincerity and godly simplicity in the denial of self, and glad endurance of privation, hardship, thanklessness, and reproach in the service of Thy poor, and the little ones of Thy flock, and such faithful perseverance in meekness, lowliness, and long-suffering, and abounding charity among each other, and to all men, as may obtain Thy merciful acceptance and overflowing blessing for their work : through the alone merits and intercession of Jesus Christ Thy Son our Lord. *Amen.*

3.

The Sisterhood of the Good Shepherd. Baltimore, Md.

THE organization known as the Sisterhood of the Good Shepherd, Baltimore, dates back in its earliest stages to January, 1856.

After various experiences and divers vicissitudes, under different pastoral relations, it became more fully organized as a Community under the rector of St. Luke's Church, Baltimore, in the year 1863, when it assumed its present name. He resigned his charge of the same, in June, 1870.

It was *not the outgrowth of work*, but of a desire to work, "to spend and be spent" for Him "who freely gave Himself for us." It grew out of a conscious want of being unable in society to give one's time and labor unreservedly to the Master's service—but with no intention of the Religious life, as understood in the Romish sense.

It had no specified aim, but simply set out to do whatever presented itself, under ministerial direction, in connection with the parish to which it belonged. The immediate result was a Parish school, and regular visiting among the sick and needy.

The original aim was so comprehensive that it can hardly be said to have enlarged its original scope, although it has been directly engaged in Hospital management, the care of private sick and poor, the charge of private and parish schools, and the conduct of an orphanage for boys.

The Sisterhood has followed no model, but thankfully receiving the experience of the most prominent kindred societies, and following its own Providential leadings, it has attained its present *status*.

The most serious obstacles to its usefulness have been those things which obstruct the usefulness of most great and good works in their inception, viz., the general inexperience of those who undertake them, and the want of general discipline and right views of authority, which makes it very difficult for Americans to live under rule and to lose individualisms in the life common to all.

The Sisterhood of the Good Shepherd is a

Society of women, electing its own officers, and originating and conducting its own operations, with its definite rules, principles and discipline.

The Sister Superior is the head of the Community, charged with its administration, and responsible for its internal order, the control of its operations and matters of detail. She is the organ of communication with the Society, to whom application must be made for the services of the Sisters, and other matters relating to its work.

The members of the Community are known as Resident Probationers, Sister Probationers, and Confirmed Sisters.

It is required of every applicant for membership with the Society that she shall reside for six months in the House, to test her fitness for the work. This constitutes the Resident Probationship.

The Sister Probationers are those who, having passed satisfactorily through this first term, are advanced to a second stage of probation, for a further test of their spirit and constancy.

The Confirmed Sisters are those who have passed through the entire period of probation.

At Home and Abroad. 155

Two full years will be required before one can enter the rank of the Confirmed, and not then unless she has attained her twenty-fifth year. Vows are not required; but no one is admitted to any rank in the Sisterhood without making a promise of obedience to its Rules, so long as she shall remain in connection with it.

Manifestly, such a calling should be undertaken "soberly, advisedly, and in the fear of GOD," and no woman should seek or accept full membership in a Community unless with the intention, deliberately reached, of devoting herself to it for life, subject only to the manifestations of GOD'S Will, and provided a fitness for it be discovered by means of a sufficiently lengthy and satisfactory probation.

The Rules make provision for releasing a member from the Society, *for cause, and upon sufficient notice.*

Persons under eighteen, cannot be received without the written consent of their Parents or Guardians.

Persons over forty-five, and widows with children, are not elegible for membership, save as Associate Sisters.

The period of probation may be lengthened, but never abridged.

The Sisters retain their Baptismal Names.

Each class of the Community wears a distinctive dress—plain and simple, but uniform.

The Sisters having "food and raiment" provided, are expected to be therewith content.

Those women whose hearts GOD may touch and move to engage in this work, should remember that the first condition for the life of a Sister must be a soul-engrossing love for GOD, and an earnest, deep desire and intention to consecrate themselves in body, soul and spirit to this holy calling. No mere considerations of convenience, taste or fancy, should lead one to engage in such a work; but there should be a hearty sacrifice and offering of oneself to the service of the Divine Master, desiring only to know His love, to do His will, to be imbued with His Spirit, and to minister to His glory.

In addition to these spiritual requirements, there should be such recognition of law and order as every corporation finds to be essential to its life, and an honest determination to observe the rules of the Sisterhood in letter and spirit.

Good health is a necessary qualification.

A stated amount for board will be expected from all those whom GOD has blessed with means, during the probationary term. The Sisters will contribute toward the general support according to their power, but in each case the amount so given is entirely at her own option, and is known only to herself, the Pastor, and the Superior.

Persons wishing to become connected with the Community should make application to the Sister Superior. They should state particulars of age, residence, such qualifications as they may think they possess, the kind of work for which they are fitted, and in general, anything relating to the motives and principles which have led them to seek a connection with the Society.

They should likewise be furnished with testimonials from their respective Pastors, setting forth their religious character and standing, and giving such particular information as will decide the propriety of encouraging a farther movement in this direction. It is especially requested that clergymen will exercise great prudence and caution in giving testimonials. Such serious interests as are involved in the work of a Sisterhood should not be jeopardized by any careless recommendations from clergymen to well-meaning women who may wish to unite with it. *Every devout and zealous Christian woman is not capable of the position, and unfit members are elements of weakness and of failure.* Great care and conscientiousness should be exercised in all such cases, and especial attention should be given to enable a Pastor to ascertain, not only the general goodness of the candidate, but likewise her probable vocation for the life in question.

The members of the Community are not at liberty to receive compensation for any services rendered, but offerings for the general fund will be gratefully accepted by the Society.

The Sisters, at present, are confined to Hospital, Educational and Orphanage work, but they know no limit to their desires, and will hold back from no good work, when by an increase of willing and efficient members, they can honestly undertake it.

The Community accepts the labors of other women who for various reasons are not able to give their whole time to its interests, under the title of Associate Sisters. They may be Resident or otherwise. It is required of them to devote a certain portion of each day or week, as may be agreed upon, to the discharge of such duty as their peculiar talents fit them for, under the direction of the head of the society. Resident Associates are held to be bound by the general Rules of the Community, so far as they relate to the good order and management of the household. Outside Associates, though not so bound, must be careful to lead lives becoming those who are connected with such a work of Religion and Charity.

The Sisterhood deeply needs the sympathy and prayers of GOD'S people, but above all things else, the services of earnest-hearted, true women, who for the Master's sake will cast in their lot with it, and consent to "spend themselves and be spent" in a privileged life of self-devotion.

Communications touching the Sisterhood, or its works, may be addressed to "The Sister Superior, Church Home and Infirmary, *Broadway, Baltimore.*"

PRINCIPLES AND RULES

OF THE

SISTERHOOD OF THE GOOD SHEPHERD.

The following RULES have been adopted to aid the Sisters in leading lives of prayer, watchfulness, self-denial, humility, and simple trust in the LORD JESUS CHRIST.

May He, from whom alone proceed all holy desires, all good counsels, and all just works, grant that, seeing and knowing what things we ought to do, we may have grace and power faithfully to fulfil the same, through Jesus Christ our Lord. *Amen.*

RULES.

1. No person shall be admitted as a Confirmed Sister under the age of 25, nor over that of 45 years; or as a probationer for membership with this Sisterhood under the age of 18, without the consent of her parents or guardians.

2. The ordinary period of probation shall be two years—six months of which shall be passed as a Resident Probationer, and the remainder of the time as Sister Probationer.

3. The object of the Resident Probationers during their six months of residence, is to test their spirit, constancy and fitness for the work. This introductory period having been satisfactorily passed, they may be admitted as Sister Probationers, and shall then make a promise of obedience to the Rules of the Community in the Chapel of the House.

4. After having passed satisfactorily through the full probationary term of two years, the candidate may be admitted as a full or Confirmed Sister. She shall then renew her promise of obedience to the rules of the Society, and shall receive the benediction of the Bishop or Spiritual head of the Community.

5. While it is to be supposed that every applicant for probation deliberately intends to devote herself to the service for life, yet experience, or the call of God's providence, may prove the expediency of a voluntary withdrawal or a dismissal from the Community. In case of voluntary withdrawal, unless there is good reason for haste, a notice of three months will be required by the Superior.

Dismissal will require a two-third vote of the Community in Chapter assembled.

6. The Sisters shall preserve their own Baptismal names.

7. The Sisterhood shall retain its present simple uniform, which can be changed only by a two-third vote of the Confirmed Sisters.

8. It is expected that the probationers, on entering the Society, and the Sisters during their connection with it, shall contribute according to their ability for the maintenance of the Sisterhood. The amount thus given shall be known only to the person herself, the Superior, and the Pastor.

9. The work of the Sisterhood shall be distributed among the Sisters by the Superior, according to their individual capacity, as far as possible.

10. Each Sister shall receive from the Superior a time-table, in which the order and arrangement of her daily work, reading, &c., shall be definitely fixed.

11. The Sisters and Probationers shall give such reports of their work to the Pastor and Superior as may be required.

12. The hours for religious service in the Chapel of the house, shall be the First hour (7 A. M.) ; Third hour (9 A. M.) ; Sixth hour (12 M.); Ninth hour (3 P. M.) ; Even. Song (6 P. M.) ; and Compline (9 P. M.) It is understood, however, that the public service of the Church shall supersede any of the foregoing hours.

13. No one shall needlessly absent herself from any of these services ; and, when lawfully detained, she shall excuse herself in person or by note to the Superior.

When so detained she shall be careful to observe the hour by uniting herself in spirit with those who are then engaged in the direct worship of God.

14. The rule for division of time may be relaxed by the Superior in cases of sickness or grave emergency.

15. Every Friday evening a special service of Prayer shall be used by the Sisters in Community for a blessing on their work.

16. Silence shall be observed in going into or out of the Chapel, unless from necessary cause.

The Pastor and Superior shall have power to

appoint other times when silence shall be observed in the Sisterhood.

17. The food provided at the regular meals shall be of a plain and simple character. No remarks shall be made concerning it, and no food shall be provided out of the ordinary mealtimes except by permission of the Superior.

18. The furniture of the rooms shall be plain, simple, and, as nearly as possible, uniform.

19. The members of the Community shall, at all times, but especially in the street, be careful to observe a quiet, modest, self-contained behavior, avoiding everything that is likely to attract attention to themselves.

20. The absence of a Sister or Probationer from the Sisterhood, the direction and purpose of such absence, must be previously approved by the Superior. Each Sister shall be entitled to an aggregate of one month in every year.

21. The members of this Society, when absent from the Sisterhood, must be on their guard to lead a life becoming those who are engaged in such a work of religion and charity.

22. A written statement is to be furnished to the Superior by all who enter, giving the names

and residences of their near relatives or friends, with whom communication may be had in case of sickness, death, or any emergency.

The Sister Superior shall record this in a book, which shall be kept for the purpose.

23. A member of the Society, when absent from the Sisterhood, shall not attend any other place of worship than that of the Church.

24. Argumentative conversation on political, sectional and controversial subjects, shall be abstained from by all associated in the work.

25. The Sisters shall have free intercourse and correspondence with relatives and approved friends: provided the proper times for giving and receiving visits are observed, and all discussion of the affairs of the Sisterhood be avoided.

26. Each member of the Community is responsible for the condition of her room, which she must be careful to keep well aired and in perfect order.

27. Other Christian women, desirous of aiding the work of the Sisterhood, may occupy a definite position in the Community under the title of Associate Sisters.

Their obligations and duties are given in the Rules for Associates.

28. The members of the Community shall have allotted to them a portion of time every day for retirement and devotion, and especially for self-examination as to their obedience to the spirit of their Rule.

29. The order of precedence among the Sisters is that of the time of their reception or advancement to either rank of the Community.

30. If any Sister should have cause of complaint or discontent regarding any person or thing connected with the Community, it shall be mentioned only to the Sister Superior or to the Pastor.

31. No remuneration shall be received by any member of the community for nursing or other services rendered, either within or without the House. When any proffer of the kind is made, it must only be accepted in the name of the Society, and with the distinct understanding that it is not for individual benefit but for the general fund of the Sisterhood.

32. No general intercourse shall be held between the Sisters except in the Community Rooms, and one Sister will not be allowed to pay a visit to another without the permission

of the Sister in charge of the House. This will not prevent a Sister from going to the door of another Sister's room upon a necessary errand, or in case of serious sickness and other extreme necessity.

CONCERNING CHAPTERS.

1. Meetings for the purpose of discussing and regulating the general affairs of the Community shall be held on the first Friday in each month, at $7\frac{1}{2}$ P. M. Special meetings may be called at any time by the Superior. She may likewise omit regular meetings at her discretion, but never more than two in succession.

2. The meetings will be presided over by the Superior, or in her absence by some one appointed by her.

3. It shall require not less than half the Confirmed Sisters to form a quorum.

4. None but Confirmed Sisters shall be entitled to a vote on matters brought before the meeting.

5. In order to pass any measure, a two-third vote of the Confirmed Sisters will be required.

6. An absent Sister may vote by proxy.

7. Matters introduced merely for discussion or information, will be decided upon by the Superior;

but if a Resolution is offered, a vote must be taken.

RULES OF LIFE AND DUTY.

1. Strive to do everything for God alone, for the increase of His glory, and from pure love to Him, remembering that "if thine eye be single, thy whole body shall be full of light."

2. Make the above your first resolution at waking in the morning and the last at night.

3. Be as exact in prayer, in reading, and in examination of conscience, as in taking your bodily nourishment.

4. If hindered from these acts at your regular hour, try if possible to find time for them afterwards.

5. Do all acts of duty, small or great, as perfectly as you can. The intention and the will gives the real value to every action.

6. At all times desire to be divested of self-will and selfishness, and with entire simplicity to be conformed to the will of JESUS only.

7. In all your annoyances and discouragements strive to rise above them, and never make them the subject of general discussion or complaint, unless in Chapter assembled.

8. Never allow anything but duty or absolute necessity to keep you from the offices of Prayer in Church or in Community; and if so detained, be careful to unite yourself in intention with your Sisters who are engaged in the more direct worship of GOD.

HOLY COMMUNION.

1. Prepare for Holy Communion by careful self-examination, contrition, and an earnest determination to correct whatever is amiss in your character.

2. When called upon suddenly to receive, strive, in the short space of time allowed you, to make as full a preparation as you can.

3. Cherish a desire for union with our LORD—fix on some especial grace to be asked for, and some especial offering to be made to GOD.

4. Take pains to avoid the fault and to practice the virtue that you have particularly intended to get rid of, or to acquire.

5. Remember that it is your privilege and duty to open the grief to your Spiritual Guide, which may at any time deter you from the LORD'S Table.

6. Cultivate at all times habits of reverence,

but avoid display in your devotions. Practices more extreme than those now generally used, will not be sanctioned in the services of the Church or Community.

OF TEMPTATIONS.

1. Resist them promptly but calmly; look at once and with entire confidence to our Blessed LORD.
2. During the conflict, commit yourself in trustful love to the LORD JESUS CHRIST.
3. Exercise the deepest humility, and fear not the power of the tempter, while you remember that greater is He that is with you, than he that is against you.
4. Distrust yourself, but trust in CHRIST.
5. Guard against the occasions of temptation. Learn by self-examination where your weak point is, and strengthen it by especial watchfulness and prayer.

AFTER A FAULT.

1. Never be discouraged, dismayed, or perplexed.
2. Acknowledge and renounce your fault calmly, sincerely, and lovingly, trusting for forgiveness,

even if it have occurred many times the same day.

3. Let this acknowledgment be open, if the fault were against others; secret, if concerning yourself.

4. This acknowledgment being made, and a full purpose of amendment formed, believe the fault to be pardoned, and that the pardon will be sealed in the next absolution.

5. Set yourself to do what before you had failed to do, and do it in the best manner you can.

6. No Sister shall resort to the extreme remedy of "Sacramental Confession" without informing the Superior of her intention so to do. This will in no wise restrict her liberty in seeking spiritual counsel, direction and advice, from her pastor.

IN THE WORK.

1. Punctuality at services, meals and other stated times, must be observed whenever practicable.

2. Be more desirous to do the will of another than your own.

3. In each department submit to her who is at the head of it, as to the delegate of the Superior.

4. Be content to take the lowest place.

5. Labor diligently and obediently.

6. Never interfere with the work of the other Sisters, nor go into their department, except in cases of necessity or by permission.

7. Guard against meddlesomeness, remembering that you are responsible only for your own work, and have no business to look after that of another.

8. Refrain from censuring another Sister's work.

9. Always be ready to report to the Superior the condition of the work assigned to you.

10. As you will assuredly meet with many things to try and fret you in your work, remember that you are not called to a life of ease and self-pleasing, but to one of self-denial and self-discipline.

Receive, therefore, all the annoyances and vexations you may encounter as so many opportunities for growth and advancement in a holy life.

Consider that "even CHRIST pleased not Himself," and that if you would indeed be His disciple, you must take up your cross daily and follow Him.

11. The Sister in charge of a department or class is alone to give orders concerning it.

12. Always support one another's authority, and never express an unfavorable opinion of another Sister's order.

13. In giving an order, or quieting a disturbance, be careful that your own looks, words and manner, express complete self-control.

14. Do not argue with children or persons under your care; give the order, and if objections are raised, enforce silence by saying "hush," or "it is against rule."

15. Always avoid irritating expressions, and in reproof rather urge the obligation of the rule than give a fresh order as of yourself.

16. Do not assume an affronted tone with those under your care, or let them see they have power to annoy you.

17. Avoid familiarities, and preserve a constant, humble dignity, while showing the utmost kindness, gentleness and sympathy of spirit.

18. On commencing any work, or entering the work-room, and often during your occupations, make an offering of them to God, and use short, secret prayers for help.

In outside ministrations do not exceed the time allotted to you, except in cases of imperative urgency.

19. To avoid embarrassment to the Society, the Sisters must be careful to temper their zeal with discretion, and not go beyond their own strength, for the means and appliances of the Sisterhood; neither shall they apply to individuals outside of the Community for aid without permission.

IN COMMUNITY.

To the Sister Superior.

1. Receive her directions cheerfully and follow them faithfully. Even should they prove unwelcome or disagreeable, let there be no murmuring or complaint.

2. Never discuss her directions, canvass her motives, find fault with her, or throw disrespect on her authority.

3. Guard against injurious suspicions or insinuations as to her motives or conduct, and do not indulge in unkind or disparaging remarks concerning her.

4. After informing her of anything you may consider wrong, be satisfied there to leave the matter;

your responsibility is over; it is her place to decide and amend what needs correction.

5. Regard her as your counsellor and friend, and believe that she has the good of the Community as much at heart as you can possibly have.

TO COMPANIONS.

1. "Whatsoever ye would that men should do to you, do ye even so to them."

2. Cultivate the spirit of Divine charity, which is the very "bond of peace and all virtues."

3. Bear all from your companions without giving them anything to bear from you.

4. Never make unkind or mortifying remarks, and avoid alluding to any peculiarities of character, appearance, or disposition.

Shun partizanship, and always speak to and of them in a spirit of kindness and love.

5. Judge nothing rashly, hastily, or unkindly.

6. In your desire for mutual service, do not go beyond your allotted sphere of duty; never interfere with the duties of another.

7. Be courteous in all your intercourse with your companions. Study to be kind, obliging, gentle and forbearing.

8. Let your language always be gentle and respectful, and remember that a "low voice is a pleasant thing in a woman."

9. Do not harbor resentment, unkindness or bitterness, towards any who may hurt your feelings or cause you pain.

10. Never blame a companion unless it be the duty of your office to do so.

11. Pray for all your Sisters daily.

12. In recalling a Sister to order, let it be sufficient to say, "it is against rule."

CONCERNING INTERCOURSE WITH SOCIETY.

1. Let your intercourse with those outside the House be modest, cheerful, gentle, reticent and edifying.

2. Be careful neither to speak nor write of the domestic or other occurrences of the House, unless duty or charity require it.

3. Avoid idle conversation touching the Sisterhood, its rules, its duties, or its prospects.

4. Do not relate what you have heard within the Community, unless it is something edifying.

5. Observe carefully the appointed times for giving and receiving visits.

6. Each Sister shall be entitled to part of a day in each week for visiting or other relaxation.

IN RECREATION.

1. Do not allow any proud or overbearing tone in thought or word.
2. Avoid all unseemly jesting, and especially never make the word of God the subject of any light remark.
3. Cherish refinement, politeness, and marked attention toward each other.
4. Contribute towards the general happiness by the serenity of your countenance and the cheerfulness of your conversation.
5. Leave the recreation the moment the time comes for any duty.
6. Remember that Christians are temples of the Holy Ghost, and that great reverence and respect are due to each other, not only for politeness, but also for religion's sake.
7. Do not absent yourself from your Associates during Community hours, except when it is necessary, and then only by permission from the Superior.

CONCERNING ASSOCIATES.

1. The appointment of Associates depends upon a two-third vote of the Confirmed Sisters, of which they shall be notified by the Superior. The Pastor will welcome them to the Society at one of the services of the Chapel.

2. Candidates for Resident Associateship will be required to pass through a six months' test before being formally admitted as such.

3. They are required to state the number of hours they will devote daily or weekly to the service of the Community, and the kind of work they will undertake to perform under the direction of the Superior, to whom they will report the result at such intervals as may be agreed upon.

4. They shall have the privilege of admission to the Chapel whenever they desire it ; and shall be especially remembered in the prayers of the Community.

5. They are on their part bound to offer up certain prayers for the prosperity of the Sisterhood, and in all proper ways to advance its interests.

6. Resident Associates are held to be bound by the general Rules of the Community, so far as they relate to the good order and management of the household, and are required to wear an appointed habit.

Outside Associates, though not bound by the above provisions of this rule, must be careful to lead lives becoming those who are associated in such a work of Religion and Charity.

4.

Order of Deaconesses of the Diocese of Alabama.

IN CHARGE OF THE CHURCH HOME, MOBILE, ALA.

THIS Order was organized at Mobile, Alabama, in the year 1864, by the Rt. Rev. R. H. Wilmer, D.D., Bishop of the Diocese. Originally it consisted, to use the Bishop's words, " of three godly women," who associated themselves under the Bishop's direction, and supervised for whatever work might be assigned to them. Their first work was the care of an Orphanage and Boarding-school for girls,—separate establishments, but under one head. The Orphanage increased so rapidly that it was found necessary to give up the Boarding-school and devote the energies of those associated exclusively to the Orphanage, with the ultimate aim of extending the work until it should include a School, Infirmary, Orphanage, Widows' House, and Reformatory Asylum. At present there is a day-school connected with the Orphanage.

The Association now numbers five Deaconesses, one Probationer, and two resident Associates, having under their charge thirty-one orphan children, some of whom are infants, and most of whom are very young.

All the work in the Church Home is done by the inmates, there being no hired service of any kind. The Bishop is the Head and Rector, with adequate alternate pervision, as indicated by the Constitution of the Order, which follows.

CONSTITUTION AND RULES.

1. This Order of Christian women, under the pastoral care of the Bishop of the Diocese, is established for the management of Infirmaries, Asylums, etc., the formation of Parish Training and other Church Schools ; and such other works of charity as may be deemed expedient.

2. The members of this Order are divided into three classes—1st, Deaconesses—2d, Probationers—3d, Associates.

3. The Deaconesses are those who, having

passed their probationary term, are admitted upon application to the Bishop, by a vote of not less than two-thirds of the Deaconesses, according to regulation. After which they are assigned to duty by the Bishop. They must be twenty-one years of age.

4. There shall be a Chief-Deaconess, who shall be appointed to that office by the Bishop, from one or more Deaconesses, who shall be nominated by them, and in whom shall be vested the government and regulation of the Order, and who shall assign an outline of duty to each member of the Order.

When the Bishop appoints a Chief-Deaconess, he shall also appoint a Vice-Deaconess, to set in place of the former, when necessity requires.

5. The Deaconesses shall assume a uniform, according to regulation.

6. Every Deaconess shall be provided with —— sum of money, annually, for her personal expenses, while in active service; and during sickness and old age, she is in all things provided for at the expense of the Order.

7. Every Deaconess is forbidden to receive fee or compensation for her services. Whenever

remuneration is made, it must be paid to the Order, and placed in its funds.

8. A Deaconess is at liberty to retire from the Order six months after having advised the Bishop of her resignation ; which time he may shorten, if he sees fit. He also has a right to dismiss any Deaconess, when, from improper conduct, or from any other grave consideration, he may deem the measure necessary.

9. There shall be stated hours of Prayer, and preparation for Holy Communion, according to regulation.

10. All the Deaconesses are entitled to an annual season of rest and freedom from care, at the discretion of the Chief-Deaconess.

11. Probationers are received for a year or more, and placed under charge of a Deaconess, in order to be fitted for the department they are expected to fill. During the probationary term, they form part of the family, and in all things conform to its rules and regulations.

12. Any one wishing to become an Associate, must hand in her name to the Chief-Deaconess, with the time she wishes to devote to the work, for report to the Bishop. If approved by the

Bishop, she may become an Associate, either Detached, for work abroad, or in Connection. A Detached Associate shall be subject to the directions of the Bishop and Chief-Deaconess, under such conditions, in each case, as shall be agreed upon at the time of admission. An Associate in Connection, must be approved by the vote of the Deaconesses, on nomination by the Bishop. Associates in Connection shall, when practicable, meet daily, for the purpose of United Prayer, and for receiving directions for their work from the Chief-Deaconess, to whom they are in all things to refer, as the head of the Order, and to whom they shall render a full report once a month.

13. It shall be the aim of the whole Order to increase its operations by an extension of the various departments of works of charity, as contemplated in Article 1.

14. The general pastoral care and spiritual direction of the Deaconesses being in the Bishop, he may delegate its mediate discharge for any portion or portions of the whole body, as he shall think proper, to one or more presbyters, as Vice-Rector or Pastor; one only, in each case, having

charge of the definitely assigned member or members of the Order, whether Deaconesses, Probationers or Associates. To such Vice-Rector or Pastor the Deaconesses are held to render deference and obedience as to the Bishop himself.

15. There shall be a Treasurer of the Order, appointed by the Bishop, who shall keep an accurate account of the funds received, and pay them out to the Order of the Chief-Deaconess, acting under the direction of the Bishop.

16. A Chapter, consisting either of all the Deaconesses, or of representatives from each branch of the Order, shall be held at least once in three years, at such time and place as shall be designated by the Bishop.

17. No article of this Constitution shall be changed, except by the Bishop, on the expressed wish of three-fourths of the Deaconesses in Chapter assembled.

OF ASSOCIATES.

1. Besides the Confirmed or Full Sisters, Sister Probationers, and Resident Probationers, other Christian women desirous of aiding the work of

the Sisterhood, may be associated with the Sisters under the title of Associates.

2. The appointment of Associates shall rest with the Pastor and Chief-Deaconess, having the consent of the Confirmed Sisters of the Community.

3. Their appointment shall be notified to them by the Chief-Deaconess, and as soon thereafter as may be convenient, they shall be welcome to the society by the Pastor, at one of the services of the Chapel.

4. They are required to state what kind of work they will undertake to perform under the direction of the Chief-Deaconess, and they shall report to her the results at such intervals as may be agreed upon.

The following modes of assistance are suggested as most useful, viz.:

To provide or make clothing for the poor.
To collect alms.
To procure work, or promote its sale.
To teach in the schools.
To assist in music, or other classes.
To relieve the destitute.
To minister to the sick.

To visit and instruct the ignorant.

To attend to funeral arrangements for the poor.

To take charge of, or assist in the decoration of the Church.

5. They shall have the privilege of admittance to the Chapel whenever they desire it, and shall be especially remembered in the prayers of the Community.

6. They are, on their part, bound to offer up certain prayers for the prosperity of the Sisterhood, and in all proper ways to advance its interests.

7. It is expected that they will use great circumspection in speaking of the Community, its interests, prospects and working, and avoid all unnecessary and indiscriminate discussion of its affairs.

8. Though not bound by all the Rules of the Community, yet, as connected with it, they must be careful to lead lives becoming those who are associated in such a work of Religion and Charity.

RULES FOR ADMISSION INTO THE SISTERHOOD.

1. The members are understood to be animated by the spirit of the Constitution of the Order; their connection with the Sisterhood arising not simply from convenience, but from a deep, conscientious conviction that they can in this way more effectually work for the glory of God and the good of mankind.

2. No person under the age of twenty-one years shall be received as a Probationer, without the written consent of her parents or guardians.

3. The Probationary period shall be one year or more; six months of which shall be passed as Resident Probationer, the remainder as Sister Probationer.

4. Every member of the Home is under the rules of the House.

Resident Probationers having satisfactorily passed the time allotted (five months) to test their spirit, constancy and fitness for the work, shall in the Oratory solemnly sign a promise of conforming to the rules, before being received as Sister Probationers.

5. Sister Probationers, having satisfactorily

passed their Probation, may be admitted as Sisters by the benediction of the Bishop or spiritual Head—first renewing her promise of obedience.

6. The Sisters retain their baptismal name. Their dress shall be the uniform adopted. Probationers shall wear plain apparel as directed by the Chief-Deaconess.

7. Each member on entering shall furnish for record the address of near relatives and friends.

RULES—HOME LIFE.

1. Hours for Chapel service are the First Hour, Sixth Hour (12 M.) Compline (9 P. M.); any of which, however, shall be superseded by the public service of the Church.

2. Every member of the Community will be present at these services, unless prevented by appointed duty—when otherwise absent she will excuse herself by note.

3. Compline on Fridays shall be devoted to preparation for the Holy Eucharist and special prayer for a blessing on their work.

4. The Church days of fasting and abstinence shall be duly observed.

5. The offices used in the Sisterhood shall be approved by the Rector.

6. Probationers and Sisters shall contribute to the maintenance of the Sisterhood. The amount thus given shall be made known only to those in authority.

7. The Chief-Deaconess shall, as far as possible, divide the work into distinct departments, and in the distribution have regard to the fitness of each Sister.

8. A table of daily work, reading, &c., shall be furnished each Sister.

9. Time fixed for the various duties of the house, shall be adapted to the different seasons of the year.

10. Rules for division of time may be relaxed in emergencies by the appointed officer.

11. Unless prevented by appointed duty or sickness, the members will be present at the hour of meals; the regular diet shall be simple and wholesome; no remarks shall be made concerning it.

12. The furniture shall be, as near as possible, uniform.

13. Each member shall see that her room is

well aired and in order, and it shall be open to inspection.

14. No member shall visit another's room or receive visitors in her own, unless on a call of duty.

15. There shall be no unnecessary talk concerning work, nor shall annoyances, discouragements and grievances be discussed, save with the Chief-Deaconess, or with the Rector.

16. Intercourse and correspondence with relatives shall be without surveillance. The private affairs of the Sisterhood shall not be topics of correspondence. Entertainments and visitors (special cases excepted) shall be expected only at appointed hours.

17. Conversation on political and sectional subjects shall be avoided.

RULES FOR INTERCOURSE WITH THE WORLD.

1. While on the streets, the members shall be quiet and modest and self-contained in their demeanor.

2. The regular period of times of absence shall be directed by the Chief-Deaconess. During

absence the deportment of the members shall reflect a Sister Vocation.

3. No member of the house shall, present or absent, attend any other Public Worship than that of the Church.

4. No remuneration shall be received—unless with the avowed understanding that it is to go into the common fund.

5. Promiscuous visiting being incompatible with home duties—members of the "Home" will visit only at the discretion of the (acting) Chief-Deaconess.

Order of Deaconesses in the Diocese of Alabama.

RECEPTION OF A PROBATIONER IN THE CHURCH HOME, MOBILE, ALABAMA.

THE Candidate for admission as a *Probationer*, having been allowed by the Rector and Sisterhood to offer herself as a Candidate, shall, at the first midday service thereafter, be presented in the Oratory, to the Rector of the "Order," by the Chief-Deaconess, as one who desires to enter the "Home" as a *Probationer*, in the following words:

"Rev. Father in God" (if the Rector be the Bishop) or "Rev. Rector" (if the Rector be a Presbyter) "this person desires to be admitted *Probationer* for the Order of Deaconesses, in the Diocese of Alabama.

¶ *Then shall the Rector say to the Candidate (standing before him):*

"Before receiving you as a Probationer of the Order of Deaconesses, it is meet and proper that we should be certified of your full acquaintance with the Constitution and rules of the Order into which you seek admission as a Probationer; and, also, of your willingness to submit yourself to the requirements thereof, in the same way, and as fully, as if you were a *Deaconess* in the full connection.

¶ *The Deaconess appointed thereunto by the Rector, shall read aloud the Constitution and Rules of the Order, and then the Rector shall ask the Candidate:*

"Will you, whilst a Probationer of the Order, render a cheerful obedience to the requirements of the Constitution and rules just read in your hearing?"

¶ *She shall answer,*

"I will so do, the Lord being my Helper."

¶ *Then shall the Rector say,*

"The Lord, who hath given you the desire and the will to separate yourself from the world for the sake of becoming a Probationer in the Order of Deaconesses, grant you His grace, that you may be able to bring the same to good effect."

¶ *Then let the Rector, commending the Probationer to the prayers of the Deaconesses and Probationers present, begin the regular Midday service; and, just before the closing prayer, pray as follows:*

"O Almighty and most Merciful Father, who

hast ordained the services of angels and men in a wonderful order, and dost design to accept the services of all who seek to set forth thy Glory and to advance the interests of thy Kingdom; look down, we beseech Thee, with Thine eye of favor upon this, Thy servant, who, following the example of holy women of old, in giving herself to the ministry of want and suffering, desireth most earnestly Thy grace and heavenly benediction. Fill her, O Lord, with the spirit of obedience and holy fear, that she may be replenished with wisdom and endued with innocency; and be enabled by Thy grace so faithfully to do her duty in this state of probation, that she may be prepared to do all Thy holy will, and be found ever acceptable in Thy sight, O Lord, our Strength and our Redeemer. *Amen.*

¶ *Then, after the prayers, let the admitted Probationer advance and sign in a book, kept for that purpose, the promise of obedience whilst a Probationer.*

¶ *Should the Rector be absent upon the admission of a Probationer, let the Chief-Deaconess take his place, and ask the questions and use the prayers as above written.*

OFFICE OF INSTITUTION OF A DEACONESS.

¶ *Morning Prayer, or such preliminary services as shall be appointed by the Bishop, being ended, the Chief-Deaconess shall advance to the Chancel rail with the Probationers to be admitted Deaconesses, and shall say to the Bishop (if he be present and officiating):*

"Rev. father in God, I present unto you this our Sister, who, following the example of devout women, recorded in Holy Scripture, and written of in primitive times, desires to devote herself to the relief of the suffering and destitute, and comes forward to ask your benediction and the prayers of the Church, that she may have grace to do her duty as becometh so honorable and difficult a vocation."

¶ *Then shall the Bishop say:*

"Dearly beloved in the Lord, who art minded to take upon you this service in the Church of God, have you duly considered how weighty an undertaking this is, which you propose to yourself, and are you prepared, with a willing mind, to take upon you this office of ministering unto the suffering and needy?"

¶ *Then the Candidate shall say,*

"I have so considered it, and, God being my Helper, I am resolved to enter upon its duties."

¶ *The Bishop shall then say:*

Our help is in the Name of the Lord.
Response. Who hath made heaven and earth.
Bishop. Blessed be the Name of the Lord.
Response. Henceforth, world without end.
Bishop. Let us pray.

"O God, who didst of old teach the hearts of Thy faithful people, by sending to them the light of Thy Holy Spirit, grant unto this, Thy servant, by the same Spirit, to be enabled to perceive and know what things she ought to do, and to have grace and strength evermore to do the same; direct her mind in all times of doubt and perplexity; strengthen her to bear the trials of her faith and patience; comfort her in times of sorrow; cheer her when faint and weary in the way; and O God, the Holy Ghost, the Comforter and the Sanctifier of the faithful, bestow upon her Thy manifold gifts of grace—the spirit of wisdom and understanding; the spirit of counsel and ghostly strength; the spirit of knowledge and true godliness; and fill her, O Lord, with the spirit of Thy holy fear and love, now and forever. In every manifestation of Thy spirit give her grace to profit withal, for the edification of herself and the benefit of those whom she serves in Thy Name; let Thy holy love, abounding towards her more and more, stir up her heart to greater deeds of love to Thee, and to greater deeds of love to all who need her service. And upon all the members of this Order bestow Thy grace and heavenly benediction; enable them to bear each others' burdens, and thus fulfil the law of Christ our Saviour. Make them to know and feel their oneness in the mystical body of Thy dear Son, so that their fellowship here in works of love may prove to them a blessed discipline, and thus prepare them at last for the society of Thy redeemed ones in heaven: through Jesus Christ our most blessed Lord and Saviour. *Amen.*

O Almighty and everlasting God, who dost vouchsafe to accept and bless the services of those who serve Thee with a willing mind, grant, we beseech Thee, to this Thy handmaiden, such willingness of heart, such humility and quietness of spirit, such sure trust and confidence in Thy love and favor, such simplicity and sincerity in the denial of self, and such patient endurance of privation, hardship, thanklessness and reproach in the service of the poor and the little ones of Thy flock, as may obtain Thy merciful acceptance and overflowing blessing, through the alone merits of Jesus Christ, Thine only Son, our Lord and Saviour. *Amen.*

¶ *Then standing up, the Bishop shall address to the Candidates the following Exhortation:*

Dearly beloved in the Lord, I *greet you* in the *Name of the Lord!* Blessed be his Holy Name, that He hath given unto you an hearty desire to glorify Him by consecrating yourself to the holy service for which you are now set apart.

The way and means to a successful discharge of your duties is, first to consider the dignity and honor of your holy calling. For God calleth you to no less an office than to be a co-worker with Himself, in his work of mercy and benevolence to our fallen race. In doing the works of mercy and charity, you are associated with the holy men and women of all ages, who have ministered unto the poor and suffering. Nor only so, but you are joined in companionship and work even with the blessed angels, whose employment and delight it is to minister unto the heirs of salvation.

This is a great honor, indeed, that God confers upon you, in accepting your services in that work of mercy which the adorable Son of God Himself undertook to accomplish, and which the ever Blessed Spirit is ceaselessly carrying on, through the "manifold services of men and angels constituted in a wonderful Order."

But that you may live in the abiding sense of your holy calling, it is needful that you should cultivate in an especial manner the *habit of devotion*. Learn to look upon your office from the height of eternity, not to estimate it by the judgment of the world, but by the judgment which God Himself has revealed in His Holy word; wherein He declares that, "He that winneth souls is wise, and he that turneth many unto righteousness, shall shine as the stars forever and ever."

Should you be tempted to look away from the great end of your holy service, and seek to please yourself, either by coveting ease or reputation, or by rebelling against the needful rules and restraints which are made to govern you in your relations to your fellow-workers, then you will be shorn of your strength, and grow weary in well-doing ; and the work committed to your trust, will suffer through your negligence and folly

But He who hath called you is faithful, and will not suffer you to be tempted above that you are able to bear. He calleth His servants to no duty without giving the needful grace to discharge it. This thought should ever inspire you with hope. But in giving us the rewards of our labors, He worketh according to His own good will and pleasure. This thought should teach you to "wait upon the Lord with *patience;* that, after having done the will of God, you should inherit the blessing ;" and, as is testified in another place, "If we hope for that we see not, then do we with patience wait for it."

These admonitions, dear Sister, which apply to all Christian people, address themselves with a peculiar significance to those who, like yourself, are separated to a work that demands an unusual degree of faith and patience.

Therefore, continually calling to mind the dignity and responsibility of your calling, and remembering the "cloud of witnesses" who, having fulfilled their course, do now rest from their labors, "run with patience the race that is set before you, looking unto Jesus, the Author and Finisher of your faith ; who, for the joy that was set before Him, endured the cross, despising the shame, and is now set down at the right hand of the throne of God." "For consider Him that endured snch contradiction of sinners against Himself, lest you be wearied and faint in your minds."

Great need will you have daily to "consider Him"—Christ, your great Exemplar. For inasmuch as you follow Him in His labor of love, you must be a follower of His patience. The secret of your strength will be, that you look not to the world,—which cannot fully take in the tenor of your mission—not even to those for whom you labor, for they cannot comprehend your work of disinterested love—but to the Blessed Jesus, from whom you receive the spirit to work in your calling, whose example you must follow, and whose cross you must bear.

You cannot be all that you would, but you may so live as to win the commendation, which the Lord gave to one of old, "*She hath done what she could !*" And, remember, to your great and endless comfort, that God rewardeth us not only for what we do, but for what we purpose and try to do.

These things, if you will earnestly consider,—calling daily upon God for help—you will be strengthened to do your work, and finally receive the joyful benediction, "Well done, good and faithful servant; enter thou into the joy of thy Lord."

¶ *(Address to all the Deaconesses present.)*

"See that you love each other with pure hearts, fervently." Yield a ready obedience to those who are over you in the Lord. With one heart and mind strive together for the good of those committed to your care. Seek to emulate the deeds of those holy women, who helped the Holy Apostles in their ministry to the poor and needy.

Love not self,—love God. "Seek first the kingdom of God and His righteousness, and all things needful shall be added unto you." Which may God grant unto you, for His dear Son's sake.

¶ *Let us pray.*

Almighty God, the giver of all good things—who of Thy great goodness dost vouchsafe to accept the services of these Thy servants in Thy Holy Church, make them, we beseech Thee, O Lord, to be modest, humble and constant in their ministration ; to have a ready will in observing all spiritual discipline ; that they, having always the testimony of a good conscience, and continuing ever stable and strong in Thy Son Christ, may so well behave themselves in this inferior ministry to the suffering upon earth, that they may be found worthy to reign with Thee in thy Heavenly Kingdom, through the same, thy Son, Jesus Christ, our most Blessed Lord and Saviour, to whom be glory and honor, world without end. *Amen.*

BENEDICTION.

"God the Father, God the Son, God the Holy Ghost, bless, preserve, and keep you! The Lord lift up the light of His countenance upon you! The Lord prosper the work of His hand upon you. May goodness and mercy follow you all the days of your life, and may you dwell in the House of the Lord forever. *Amen.*

¶ *Then followeth the celebration of the Holy Communion.*

5.

The Sisterhood of St. Mary, of the Diocese of New York.

THE Sisterhood of St. Mary was organized February second, the Feast of the Purification, 1865. At that time five Sisters were admitted to profession, by the Bishop of the Diocese, the service being held in St. Michael's Church, Bloomingdale.

They took charge of the House of Mercy in September, 1863, a year and a half before their formal organization, and still have the care of that Institution. In October, 1864, at the request of the Rev. Dr. Peters, they undertook the opening of a Home for children, since known as the Sheltering Arms, and carried on the work until March, 1870, when they resigned it to other hands.

In June, 1865 they took charge of St. Barnabas House, Mulberry-street, and for two years, until June, 1867, had the care of that charity.

In 1868 they opened the boarding and day

school for young ladies now located at No 8 East Forty-sixth street, and known as St. Mary's School. This school numbers at present one hundred and twenty-five pupils. In the autumn of 1870 they started St. Mary's Hospital for Children, 206 West Fortieth-street.

The Sisterhood has lost two of its members by death, and now numbers twenty-two Sisters, two Postulants, two Associate Sisters, and twenty-four Associates.

The object sought in the formation of this Sisterhood was to secure the means of a complete, unreserved, and life-long dedication of the whole being to the service of Almighty God, through ministration to the poor, the needy, and the ignorant, for the love of our Lord Jesus Christ, and to the glory of his Holy Name. At first a scheme somewhat general in character was adopted ; the movement was regarded as experimental and tentative ; the idea was to learn by degrees, and to make rules and regulations as they should be needed. It was thought that, in this country, and under our peculiar circumstances, it is safer to feel the way and be taught by experience, than to begin with a rigid system which might retard or prevent growth.

Of the mechanism intended to secure the great object sought by the Sisters, there is little to be said, save that it is simple, elastic, and practical; not stiff, complicated, or theoretic. No one under eighteen years of age can be admitted to probation. No one under twenty-five years of age can be admitted to profession. A term of probation of at least two years, is required in every case: it is generally longer, often very much longer. The government is constitutional; the constitution is a written law; and the supreme power is in the Chapter, which includes all the professed Sisters. The Superior is elected by the Chapter; they also elect other officers, as well as a Board of Trustees, to manage their business affairs wherever outside aid from business men is needed.

The Sisterhood was at first incorporated under the general act for the incorporation of charitable and religious societies: it subsequently obtained from the Legislature an amended charter with enlarged powers. Under this amended act it is able to hold so much real and personal estate as will probably be necessary for the realization of its charitable designs.

To the private devotional life of the members, great attention is given; yet always with reference to the active works of mercy to which they are especially pledged. No vows are required; it is not thought that they could add weight to the solemn purpose with which each Sister devotes herself to the work. Yet if any one desires to express in terms that purpose, more formally than she does at the time of her final reception as a professed Sister, she is not denied so simple a privilege; it is regarded as within the limits of a Christian woman's liberty.

The Sisters are scattered about in several institutions. Each house occupied by them in their work is under the charge of one of the professed Sisters, who has with her such assistants as may be necessary.

In conclusion, he by whom these brief memoranda are furnished, would add, that the Sisters, in their growth thus far, have had very little assistance from the rich of this world; they have had in their numbers not one person of wealth; the foundation has been laid in humility and faith.

Not many wise after the flesh, not many mighty, not many noble are called, as it seems, to such a life. They have in their hearts the kindliest feeling towards all who desire to serve the Lord Jesus Christ, in organized labor for His poor. There are various ways of doing this ; we cannot surely tell which is best. What must be right is to lay aside thoughts of strife and contention ; to wish each other well ; to pray for each other's success ; and conscientiously to do what seems to us right, leaving results to God, the judge of all.

The Sisterhood seek no publicity ; they only wish to serve the Lord in quietude ; they interfere with no one's work, having more than enough to do in minding their own. If God be pleased to prosper them, it is well ; if not, it shall still be well.

14

6.

Bishop Potter Memorial House.*

On the grounds of the Episcopal Hospital, corner of Front-street and Lehigh-avenue, Philadelphia, Pa.

PHILADELPHIA, *December*, 1871.

TO THE REV. H. C. POTTER, D.D.

REV. AND DEAR FRIEND—Your request for a sketch of the origin and workings of the Bishop Potter Memorial House, our successful Diocesan Training School for Women Helpers, cannot be refused by one who had the great privilege and incalculable advantage of being an intimate co-worker with your revered father during the twenty years of his episcopate.

It may be interesting and instructive to consider briefly some of the preparatory work which led to the foundation of the Institution.

Twelve years since, just after the memorable

---

* This institution is under the control of the Rt. Rev. W. B. STEVENS, D.D., as Bishop of the Diocese of Pennsylvania.

Convention at Richmond, when a Committee of one layman from each Diocese was appointed to stir up the zeal of their brethren of the laity, Bishop Potter, at my instance, as a member of that Committee, convened the rectors of our city parishes and their prominent laymen, for conference on the best means of incorporating the more neglected classes into the Church. Conference after conference revealed the fact that our Theological and Parochial systems were running in grooves too deeply worn to be turned either to the right hand or the left for aggressive Parish work, until its feasibility had been practically demonstrated. The effect of Missionary work, independent of Parochial organizations, had been fully tested during the troublous years of 1857 and 1858, when public preaching, exhortation and prayer in halls and in the streets were common throughout our city. Although a large amount of vital force was thus spent, yet, like the too free use of bodily stimulants, the result was far from satisfactory.

A work of another character was soon after this inaugurated in a manufacturing suburb of the city. Although few if any parochial ministers had faith in the movement, yet Bishop Potter's far-reaching mind enabled him rightly to estimate its value. Impregnating the family life of our long neglected and estranged people with the germs of practical Christianity, carried to their homes by intelligent, experienced and sympathizing mothers and daughters, it seems to strike at the root of a great social evil. We watched over the movement with deep interest, until it became apparent that through this agency vital and practical Christianity could be indefinitely extended, and a hitherto estranged people drawn by the cords of love to Christ and to His Church. In other parishes, district visitors had often been sent into special localities to lure people by the too free use of money or clothing, to a Church which was not congenial to independent working people, because the pews were rented, and there was a lack of Christian fellowship in the congregation. The result in such cases had been disappointing, like the attempt to insert new cloth into old garments. With the new experiment, there were no money-lures and no array of officers, the Pastor merely selecting a judicious, intelligent and experienced matron to act under his observation, with liberty to select her associate workers as needed. The basement rooms of the Church were placed at her disposal, for social, educational and industrial Mother's Meetings, and for a free Sunday Service, which the Rector established for the benefit of this hitherto estranged people.

It was soon found that instead of the supposed great gulf between independent working people and the more cultivated and intelligent class, houses and hearts were freely opened to sympathizing visitors. People who had long neglected public worship, were readily drawn, in their working clothes, to a social Mothers' Meeting, and then, after becoming thrifty, to the Sunday service, by their visitors, who made them feel that Christian fellowship and the Communion of Saints were matters of fact as well as articles of faith. It was a new revelation, that with most working people, the Church seems so strange and forbidding a place, or their adhesion to it so weak, that even communicants, removing from place to place, rarely go to another Church until sought out and welcomed.

This experiment was not an individual enterprise, to end when its projector became enfeebled, but it was thoroughly incorporated into the Church's system and life. The movement was unobtrusive, quiet, orderly, prayerful, and thoroughly churchly; therefore its growth was steady in summer and in winter, in war and in peace, until its beneficial influence was acknowledged by those who had been the most skeptical. More than eight thousand visits were annually made to five or six hundred houses, and these inexpensive home influences fed the Sunday-schools, Bible classes, Mothers' Meetings and night schools with those who had not been reached by any other instrumentality.

Bishop Potter continued to observe this aggressive work; and in a letter to me under date of March 3rd, 1861, said:

"There is much temporal relief to the poor, which alienates them from pastoral oversight, and leaves them a prey, at their own homes or haunts, to improvidence, vice, and irreligion. I value the efforts making in your parish, because they demonstrate the great value of house-to-house visitation; because they show the power of judicious Christian kindness in drawing people of every age away from idleness and sin to the Lord's House; because they tend to strengthen the tie that binds husband and wife, parents and children; because they exhibit the Church at its appropriate work of ministering at once to the bodies, the minds, the social requirements, and the spiritual need of the people; and because they show that, by engaging in such works, Christians add greatly to their own enjoyment and improvement. The growth, too, of a true feeling of brotherhood among all the members of our fold, as it respects one another, and of a clearer perception of their duty to all sorts and conditions of men, may be anticipated as an inevitable consequence. Above all, do I value the spirit of prayer which preceded and attends these efforts, and which will prove the best security for their continuance and their efficiency."

To test still further this experiment, or rather to demonstrate its feasibility under other and still more adverse circumstances, Bishop Potter authorized the use of the Chapel of the Episcopal

Hospital and its basement rooms for a similar effort to reach the homes of working people, and to draw their inmates Christward and Churchward. The experiment having been thoroughly successful in a Hospital Chapel, without a vestry, and with a Chaplain whose time is almost entirely consumed in the work of the institution, and with non-resident workers, in a field in which the Episcopal Church had never found congenial soil, the practicability of the system has surely been fully demonstrated. The success of the Hospital Mission was more rapid than that at Frankford, because experimental errors could be avoided and advantage taken of the valuable experience already gained. Inquiries from every quarter were made for minute directions as to the way in which similar work could be commenced and carried on successfully. In many cases like efforts were unsuccessful through lack of women trained to give out heart-power, and to work under authority and in harmony with the Church's system. The Bishop Potter Memorial House was established to supply this pressing need, and to perpetuate and extend at home and abroad the valuable experiences of women who solved the great problem of our Church by incorporating into her membership all sorts and conditions of men.

The following extracts from the address of the writer at the official opening of the Bishop Potter Memorial House, show how deeply the revered Bishop, whose name it bears, was impressed with the importance of the work already accomplished, and how anxious he was to have other zealous women trained for a like work, and their services organized in accordance with the principles of the Church.

"This Institution springs from suggestions made in 1862 to the Convention of the Church in his diocese by the Bishop whose name it bears. In that address Bishop Potter said: 'There are many women of education, refinement and earnest piety who yearn for a sphere in which they can work for God and for the afflicted. There are those whose characters and whose enjoyments would be vastly improved by such occupation. Everywhere, but especially among the suffering and hardened of *our* sex, does woman carry the sunshine of patience and of hope. In proportion as she has lofty Christian aims, and the delicacy which comes of refined associations, she is better qualified to command respect and inspire affection; and, in proportion as she possesses the experience and the ready resource which spring generally from nothing but *training*, will her agency be permanent and useful. We have, it seems to me, but to weigh considerations like these; we have but to remember what a vast amount of talent and hearty zeal among women waits to be employed; we have but to contrast the homes of our poor in sickness, and too often, alas! in health; our prisons, our asylums, our reformatories, our almshouses, our hospitals, *as they are, with what they might be, if pervaded with a higher feminine and religious influence*, and we shall perceive that nothing but *organization* and a wise directing spirit is needed to achieve this mighty and beneficent revolution."

At a later period, the Bishop addressed to the writer the following letter:

"Philadelphia, May 3, 1864.

"My Dear Sir: I need hardly say that the opinions which I have formerly expressed in regard to the unemployed agency of Christian women, and which I developed at some length in the Convention address in 1862, are more than confirmed by our experience. In parishes, in our Church hospital, and in more than one army hospital in this city, that agency has been employed with a skill and persistency, with a constant reference to spiritual edification and a whole-hearted consecration on the part of refined and highly-endowed ladies, which fills me with admiration and with hope. In one hospital, within eight months, I have confirmed some *forty* soldiers, the fruit mainly of the agency of two or three godly women. In another, where inmates from civil life of the humblest character are welcomed, I have seen a pervading seriousness and a general turning to religious instruction largely due to a like influence.

"In more than one parish, and especially in one with which you are connected, I have seen godless men and reckless youth who had withstood all others, yielding to the silent and persevering efforts of ladies, and demonstrating how much can be done among the most forlorn of our people through their agency. It is teaching us more and more the necessity of individualizing our appeals, of making them with all kindness and constancy, and of coupling them with fervent and believing prayer.

"'Properly trained, this agency of Woman would be most benign in all our public institutions—in our prisons, almshouses, reformatories, and asylums for the sick and afflicted of every name. God bless the noble women who have given themselves to the work! The Lord make his face to shine upon efforts to extend and systematize it; and the Good Spirit rouse our sex—too slow to engage in such works—to emulate the example.

"Yours, faithfully,
"ALONZO POTTER.
"TO MR. WM. WELSH."

In a few months after the utterance of the prayer, that the Lord would make his face to shine upon efforts to extend and systematize the work of Christian women, Bishop Potter became enfeebled by sickness, and in little more than a year he 'finished his course.' This sad blow having been followed by the sickness and necessary absence of Bishop Stephens, there was, for a season, little heart for the active extension of this work; but, as the invisible rays of the sun convey the intensest heat, so, whilst this inscrutable Providence was disheartening *man*, the Holy Spirit was the more actively vivifying this seed that the revered Bishop had planted in faith. The accredited representative of Bishop Stevens in this department was at length constrained to apply to the Board of Managers of the Hospital for the use of the adjacent mansion-house as a home for ministering women, that their number might be increased without disarranging the management of the Hospital, and that they might be trained more systematically, their services organized more thoroughly, and their sphere of operations extended.

The Board promptly granted the request, and the House will be opened in two or three months, under the direction and control of the Bishop of the Diocese. All the clerical members of the Committee of the Convention on organizing the services of Christian women, being Managers of the Hospital, the Institution will also be under their observation. The connection of the undersigned with this department of Church-work was not of his own seeking; it began at Bishop Potter's solicitation, and has continued because Bishop Stephens desired to be thus represented. It is not designed to make this institution solely, or even mainly, diocesan, but auxiliary to all the missionary organizations of the Church.

The wards of the Hospital, its dispensary, its successful mission to the working people in its vicinity, and the aggresive operations in the neighboring parishes will, under the guidance of trained workers, afford invaluable schools of instruction and practice for women who are willing to serve, either separately or unitedly, in church institutions or in missionary fields. A small band of women, now in the missionary department of the hospital, are successfully reaching the independent journeymen mechanics, manufacturers and laborers, with their families; and it is specially important that this branch of woman's work should be extended throughout our whole land, as it is with this class that the Church has hitherto signally failed, both in England and this country.

This practical training will also aid the

Foreign Missions of the Church; for surely it is important to educate the powers of women, and to test them in winning souls *here*, where all the appliances and surroundings are favorable to Christianity, before they are sent to heathen lands. It is known that in Asia, millions of women, living in the deepest degradation and in the grossest superstition, can only be approached by missionaries of their own sex; and although many are predisposed to receive the only religion that ennobles women, yet the Church has been slow to stir up the holy zeal of her daughters, and to prepare them for a mission to their heathen sisters.

Mrs. Jackson, of Milwaukee, the widow of the Rev. William Jackson, of Louisville, Ky., is to be the Lady Principal of the institution, subject to the direction and control of the Bishop; and under her charge will be placed as many suitably qualified volunteers as can be procured, accommodated, and supported, without expense to the hospital. These will be trained in teaching and in charitable work, under the direction of the Principal and such helpers as she may call to her assistance. At the expiration of six months they can leave the institution, or re-enter, to prepare, according to their aptitude or taste, for some special service in the foreign or domestic fields, or for nursing in the hospital or elsewhere.

More commodious buildings will in due time be erected near the hospital, if intelligent and zealous women freely offer their services; and then bands of missionaries, of teachers, and of nurses will no doubt be organized, and look.to the "Potter Memorial House" as their home. Whilst it is in a formative condition, it would be unwise to adopt the plans and rules of any European institution, especially such as do not harmonize with the spirit of the American Church; but no vow of celibacy will be allowed, nor without the written approval of the Bishop and of the Board of Managers of the hospital, will there be any pledge of service beyond a very limited time. A large experience proves that ladies, who are modestly doing the Church's work, are not only free from insult, but are reverenced everywhere; therefore, a distinctive dress is, in this country, an open question. Indeed, in woman's great mission to the laboring class, the most successful workers think that it would be a hindrance."

After nearly five years of successful working, it has not been found necessary to modify the original fundamental principles of the institution. A distinctive dress is still an open question, but there is a disposition to adopt some badge as a bond of union between the workers, as well as for other reasons, provided there are no marked peculiarities in the attire. The following circular will afford detailed information of the principles of the institution.

INFORMATION FOR THOSE WHO WISH TO ENTER THE HOUSE.

Any earnest communicant of the Protestant Episcopal Church, who desires to enter the Memorial House, can write to Mrs. William Jackson, 2649 North Front-street, Philadelphia, giving RESIDENCE, AGE, PHYSICAL CONDITION, REASONS FOR WISHING TO JOIN THE COMMUNITY, the names of her RECTOR and OTHERS who may have precise knowledge of her adaptation for such a position. If the applicant is deemed suitable, she will be received, and may remain six months as a probationer in either one of the departments, if she is adapted to the work; at the expiration of that time, her special line of duty will be determined.

The services of the members are gratuitous. They will have their board and lodging free of expense when it is necessary; but, as the House is supported by free-will offerings, it is hoped that each member will contribute according to her ability; if she can afford it, the full amount of the cost of her board will be expected, especially during the six probationary months. All such arrangements are confidential with the Principal, as all the members fare alike, and work to the extent of their ability in designated spheres.

The House is not intended as an asylum for the homeless or world-weary; but as a household of fresh, loving hearts, strong in all their powers to "serve the Lord with gladness."

The work is at present divided into three departments—NURSING, MISSION WORK, and PARISH SCHOOLS.

The members of this House comprise two classes—Probationers and Full Members.

The Probationers are those under training for

full membership; they must not be ordinarily under twenty-five, or over forty years of age.

The term of probation is never less than six months, but twelve months is strongly recommended. The term of engagement for full members is not less than one, nor more than three years. At the expiration of which time it may be renewed, if desired.

A schedule of work and of the time to be devoted to it is given, and all are required strictly to conform to it.

There is an allotted time daily for recreation, likewise an afternoon of every week; and, during the summer, a vacation of four weeks is allowed to Full Members.

The visits of friends can only be received in unoccupied hours.

A Divine blessing continues to descend upon the Memorial House, just as evidently as of old on Aaron's rod. Ministering women at every stage of progress, like the threefold witness of bud and flower and fruit, cluster around the parent stock, and show that in the Christian Church, God has openly accepted woman's higher ministries. The rapidly growing demand for the services of trained Christian women to lead in aggressive parish work, witnesses that the Church views their mission as divine. Few are naturally gifted with the suggestive and executive powers needed for the higher forms of aggressive work, therefore it is usually an acquired art. Few women have the experience, tact and perseverance needed in training their self-distrustful sisters, and the clergy seldom have the leisure or the qualifications required to interest, direct, and oversee beginners in their experimental training. Few parishes have all the Gospel appliances thoroughly systematized and headed by successful exemplars and accomplished teachers. By the good providence of God, the Memorial House is in this respect most highly favored; and the influences of its spiritual atmosphere and of its encouraging surroundings, so needful to inspire the timid with hope, are thoroughly appreciated by the members of that household.

All who have continued in the Memorial House for a twelvemonth, have with greater or less facility acquired the Divine art of winning souls to Christ. Women who were disheartened at the awkwardness of their first attempts, have by persevering efforts accomplished so much, that other self-distrustful beginners are encouraged by witnessing their ultimate success. They learn how to apply Christian sympathy, acts of kindness, words of encouragement, sacred music, Bible reading and prayer to individual cases. It often seems more like fable than like fact, when the mother tells of the watchful care over her sick children, or of the son or daughter drawn from the verge of ruin, or of her own rescue from the fearful condition of a backslider, by one who came in Christ's name and wrought for His sake only. Men who have been thus sought out in home, or workshop, or hospital, and savingly interested in their spiritual welfare, usually manifest the deepest interest in these heaven-sent messengers.

The Rev. George Washburn, of Constantinople, a zealous and intelligent missionary of the American Board of Commissioners for Foreign Missions, visited the Memorial House. He examined carefully the Protestant training-houses and Sisterhoods, in France, Germany, and England, and having a practical knowledge of the successes of the Deaconesses of Kaiserswerth when serving in foreign fields, he had deliberately formed an ideal of the training and organization needed by American women to give them full efficiency, either as missionaries from house to house, as teachers, or as dispensary and hospital nurses in foreign lands. Mr. Washburn "was much pleased to find, from minute inquiry and personal inspection, that his ideal had already been embodied, and was working successfully at the Bishop Potter Memorial House, where cultivated Christian women are trained by experts to work in these three departments in schools of practice; and that here, as at Kaiserswerth, the primary object in each department is to win the soul to Christ."

The Very Rev. Dean Howson, very lately expressed an equally favorable opinion, after a personal examination of the Institution.

Since the opening of the Memorial House thirty ladies have been received as Probationers; three of these were sent by the Foreign Committee of the Board of Missions to be specially trained and tested before going to heathen lands; and two belonging to other communions, were admitted to acquire experience in Christian work. There are now seven Full Sisters, and four Probationers. All who have been connected with the institution have evidently increased in Christian usefulness; and having learned to work under authority and in harmony with others, their efficiency is likely to increase still farther. There are also seven Associate Sisters, who, though not trained in the Institution, pray and work to further its great aim. Some of these form the council of advice, and others are the teachers and trainers of their less experienced Sisters.

One of the women sent by the Foreign Committee for special training at the Memorial House is connected with the African Mission; one of the Sisters is at the Santee Indian Mission in Nebraska, under the Rev. S. D. Hinman; another is at the Yankton Indian Mission, working under direction of the Rev. J. W. Cook. One was sent to inaugurate a parish of working people, and although a Church has been built and is doing efficient service, yet she cannot leave there until her co-workers have sufficient training and experience to carry on the house-to-house visiting, mothers' meetings, &c. Two others have successfully begun a similar work in a destitute region about two miles from the Memorial House. There is an almost daily demand for trained Christian women, which cannot be supplied without unduly decreasing the force required for the adjacent Hospital and Mission, and for training probationers.

The supineness of the Church in this Diocese and elsewhere, in regard to the trained and organized services of Christian women, is still so great as to need special efforts to make the members of our Communion intelligently conscious of the value of the Bishop Potter Memorial House and similar institutions.

The admirable report to the Board of Missions, prepared and read by you, will, I feel sure, aid in arousing the Church to the importance of urging her daughters to prepare for the great work to which they are now providentially called.

Yours, sincerely,
WM. WELSH.

7.
Sisterhood of the Good Shepherd, New York.

THE Sisterhood of the Good Shepherd was organized at St. Ann's Church, New York, on the second Tuesday after Easter, 1869, by the Right Rev. the Bishop of the Diocese. At the time of the organization the Sisterhood consisted of three Sisters then received, three Visitors, and one Associate. Since then one Sister has died. At present there are two full Sisters, eleven Associates, and four Visitors connected with the Sisterhood.

The work of the Sisterhood of the Good Shepherd is the care of St. Barnabas House, New York, a refuge for destitute girls and women, which also includes a Day Nursery, and a shelter for neglected children. In addition to this, the Sisters extend their labors to the poor of their neighborhood, and to Bellevue Hospital, and the hospitals on Ward's Island, where their teachings and ministrations include both Germans and English.

The following are the Principles of Organization adopted by the Sisterhood:

1. This Association shall be called "The Sisterhood of the Good Shepherd in the City and Diocese of New York."

2. Its object shall be to minister to the poor, the sick, the homeless, and the outcast, and to care for little children.

3. The Sisterhood shall be under the control of the Bishop of the Diocese, who shall be its head, and appoint its pastor.

4. The Sisterhood shall embrace five classes, Sisters, Assistants, Probationers, Visitors, and Associates, over all of whom the Presiding Sister shall have control.

The *Associates* shall be those who, residing in their own families, are able to give only a portion of their time each week or year to the work. They are expected to offer daily the prayer for the Sisterhood furnished to them.

The *Visitors* shall be those who wish to become Probationers, or those who desire to give themselves to the work for a certain time residing with the Sisters during this time.

The *Probationers* shall be those who having passed six months as Visitors, and then desiring to give themselves wholly to the work, and being approved by the Presiding Sister, shall assume the dress, and be received by the Pastor.

The *Assistants* shall be those who wish to devote themselves to work for Christ, but whose lives here have been so ordered that they are not fitted for the position of a full Sister. They shall be Probationers two years, and then, if approved by the Presiding Sister, and the Pastor, shall be received by the Pastor and take the name of Sister.

The *Sisters* shall be those, who having passed a probation of two years, and still desiring to give themselves wholly to the work, and being approved by the Presiding Sister, Pastor, and Bishop, shall then be received by the Bishop, and be known as Sisters.

5. Whenever the "Sisters' Fund" will permit, each Sister shall receive the sum of $150 each year, for personal expenses. Each Assistant

shall receive the sum of $100 each year for the same purpose.

The Presiding Sister shall be allowed discretion as to the support of the other classes, when necessary.

6. No rule shall be made by the Presiding Sister without the approval of the Pastor and Bishop.

If a majority of Sisters object to any rule, they may appeal to the Bishop, who shall annul it if he thinks best.

7. The Presiding Sister shall arrange all the work, but no new work shall be undertaken without the approval of the Pastor and Bishop.

8. The head of each House shall have the direction and control of the work, and of those engaged in it, subject only to the control of the Presiding Sister.

9. The Presiding Sister shall see that each worker has a month each year for recreation.

10. Family ties being of the most sacred obligation, any Sister may leave the work of the Sisterhood at any time that family duties require it. In such case, if she desires to continue a Sister, she may do so, with the consent of the

Presiding Sister and Pastor, returning to the work of the Sisterhood when Providence permits. But while attending to duties in, or for her family, she shall not receive the Sisters' support.

11. A Sister wishing to withdraw from the Sisterhood, shall give written notice thereof, with the reasons, to the Presiding Sister, who shall give this notice, with her own judgment in the case, also in writing, to the Bishop. The Bishop's formal sanction shall be an honorable discnarge from the Sisterhood.

But that due provision may be made for the work in which she has been engaged, such withdrawal shall not take place in less than two months after the notice has been given, unless by special consent of the Presiding Sister.

12. An Assistant may withdraw in the same manner, the Pastor taking the place of the Bishop.

13. A Probationer may withdraw at any time by giving due notice to the Presiding Sister and the Pastor.

14. With the consent of the Pastor, the Presiding Sister may, for cause, request a Probationer to withdraw at any time.

15. Probationers must not be over forty nor under twenty-one years of age, without the special consent of the Presiding Sister.

16. Regulations respecting dress, and the social ordering of the household, shall, for the present, be left entirely to the Presiding Sister, and shall not be embraced within the permanent rule, under a year's trial.

17. In case of the death or resignation of the Presiding Sister, the Sisters, after receiving the Holy Communion at the hands of their Pastor, shall give in their votes, for not less than two and not more than three names, from which the Bishop, or in case of a vacancy in the Episcopate, the Pastor, shall choose one who shall be Presiding Sister.

Until this appointment has been made, the Sister first in order of reception shall discharge the duties of the Presiding Sister.

Application for admission to the Sisterhood may be made to SISTER ELLEN, St. Barnabas House, No 304 Mulberry Street, or to the Pastor, the REV. DR. GALLAUDET, No. 9 West Eighteenth Street, New York City.

8.
Sisterhood of St. John.

IN CONNECTION WITH ST. JOHN'S PARISH, WASHINGTON, D.C.

THIS Sisterhood was organized by the Rector of St. John's Church, Washington, the Rev. John Vaughan Lewis, A.M., in December, 1867. At the outset a body of Associate Sisters was formed, and as fast as any among these have proved themselves qualified for increased responsibilities, they have been advanced to the rank of full Sisters. The Order has been devoted to works of mercy among children, the sick, and the destitute, which have been conducted with increasing and signal success.

The following are the Statutes, Rules of the Community, and Rules of the Associates:

STATUTES.

I.

1. THERE shall be three Orders of Sisters, to which any unmarried women or widows, being communicants of the Church, shall be eligible, as hereinafter provided.

2. These Orders shall be respectively known as Sisters, Probationers, and Associates; and the first two shall constitute a Community, to which the Order of Associates shall be auxiliary.

II.

It is hereby declared that no work of Charity, Mercy, or Benevolence, approved as such by the Pastor, is foreign to the objects of this Sisterhood, or any of its Orders.

III.

The government of the Sisterhood shall be vested in the Rector of St. John's Parish, as Pastor, except as hereinafter provided and limited.

IV.

The administration of the Community shall be committed to one of the Order of Sisters, or, if there be no Sisters, of Probationers, who shall be called the Superior, and whose duty it shall be to see that the rules are faithfully obeyed by all the Community.

V.

The Superior shall be appointed by the Pastor; but if his appointment be not accepted by vote of the Community within five days, then he shall appoint another in like manner. But if the second appointment be not accepted within five days, then the Pastor shall appoint absolutely.

VI.

1. All votes of the Community shall be taken in a Meeting in Chapter, of which each member has been duly warned.

2. It shall be competent for the Chapter to vote upon nominations to office, new statutes and rules, and admission to membership; and an unanimous vote only shall confirm and accept.

VII.

1. The Sisters shall promise conformity to all the rules of the Order.

2. They shall engage with the Order for a term of not less than one year, and not more than three years.

3. They may renew their engagements, with the consent of the Order.

4. They shall be entitled to receive at least one hundred dollars annually from the common fund of the Community, for their personal expenses and private charities.

5. They shall wear a uniform garb, not singular nor conspicuous.

6. They may withdraw, for cause, from the Sisterhood, upon giving two months' notice to the Pastor, and obtaining his consent and release.

7. They shall have served at least one year as Probationers before they shall be eligible as Sisters.

8. They must be at least twenty-one years of age before applying for admission, and must produce the written consent of their parents or guardians, unless they have attained the age of thirty-five years.

9. They shall be wholly supported out of the common fund of the Community.

10. In case of sickness or disability, they shall be entitled to the care and support of the Community during such disability, notwithstanding the expiration of their term of service.

VIII.

1. The Probationers shall comprise all postulants for admission to the Order of Sisters.

2. They shall conform to all the rules of the Community.

3. They shall be at least twenty years of age.

4. They shall be entitled to the same allow-

At Home and Abroad.

ance and support as the Sisters, but shall not become a charge upon the Community in case of sickness or disability.

5. They may withdraw at any time, on giving one week's notice to the pastor.

6. They shall each be placed under the guardianship and instruction of one of the Sisters, to be fitted for the departments they are expected to occupy.

IX.

1. The Superior shall hold office three years, unless sooner relieved by the Pastor.

2. She shall have the custody of the common fund of the Community, and shall render an account of the same, monthly, to the Pastor.

3. She shall advise with the Chapter and with the Pastor on all questions of finance involving more than twenty dollars; but the decision of such questions shall rest absolutely with herself.

4. She shall faithfully warn the weak and encourage the desponding; and the sick and afflicted ones of the Community shall be her especial charge.

5. She shall avoid all partiality and favoritism in the discharge of her duties.

6. She shall assign to each Sister and Probationer her daily duty; and having assigned any member to the oversight of a particular department, shall not remove her, except at the request of the member herself, or with the advice and consent of the Pastor.

7. She shall be held responsible to the Pastor for all the doings of the Community.

8. She shall observe a special season of daily prayer for herself and the community.

X.

The Common Fund of the Community shall consist of all alms which any member or other person may bestow upon the Community; of all bequests and legacies to the Sisterhood not specifically designated by the advisors; and of all fees and remunerations received by any member in recognition of her services as a member of this Community, or in recompense of the same.

XI.

1. The Associates shall consist of all such persons as are eligible under Statute I., who are willing to pledge themselves to one hour of daily work auxiliary to the objects of the Sisterhood.

2. They shall be received into the Order for a term of not less than one month, and not more than one year (being eighteen years of age, and having received the consent of their parents or lawful guardians), after an unanimous election by the Order.

3. They shall promise conformity to all the rules of the Order, and sign their names to the same in the presence of the Order.

4. They shall be governed by a separate code of rules, which shall be administered by one of their own number appointed by the Pastor and approved by a vote of the Order, and who shall be styled Associate Superior.

5. They may be re-elected at the expiration of their term of service.

6. They may be released from their engagement to the Order, (*a*) upon marriage, *ipso facto;* (*b*) upon just and reasonable cause, with the consent of the Pastor ; (*c*) upon dismissal for a flagrant breach of pledge. But no dismissal shall, in any case, be made known to any but the Pastor, the Associate Superior, and the Associate dismissed ; and the power of dismissal shall be vested in the Pastor.

XII.

1. The Pastor, with the advice and consent of the Bishop of the Diocese, may, from time to time, propose new statutes and rules to the Sisterhood.

2. No new statute or rule shall be adopted, or have any force, until it has received the unanimous consent of the Orders affected by its provisions, attested by subscription thereto; but when so adopted, it shall have all the force of the original statutes or rules.

XIII.

Nothing in these statutes or rules shall be construed so as to conflict with the authority of those to whom the Associates severally owe natural obedience.

RULES OF THE COMMUNITY.

RULE I.

Every Sister, on being received into the Order, shall make this solemn promise and pledge:

"In the Name of the Father, and of the Son, and of the Holy Ghost. Amen. I (A. B.) having been duly released from obligation to those to whom my natural obedience is due (*or*, being full thirty-five years of age), do freely, and of my own mind, make this pledge and agreement: to renounce and put away the world, its secular business and engagements, that I may the more humbly and entirely serve Christ Jesus my Lord in the fellowship and obedience of this Order of Sisters of the Sisterhood of St. John, to which I now seek admission.

"And I do promise and engage that I will conform to and abide by the Statutes and Rules of this Sisterhood, so far as they relate to my Order, or my office therein, without murmuring or remonstrance.

"And I do further promise and engage that, in all my work for Christ in this my Order, I will obey the directions of the Superior cheerfully and to the best of my ability, and that I will not seek to be released from this my engagement before the expiration of my term of service, without urgent necessity, and special prayer for guidance.

"And I do further promise and agree that I will never ask or seek from any person any other recompense or recognition, by reward, of my services than that which is now, or may hereafter, be allowed me by the Statutes and Rules of the Sisterhood; and that, should any such recompense, fee or payment be offered me, I will receive it only in the name of the Sisterhood, and for the common fund of the Community.

"And I do further promise and agree that I will cultivate peace, love, and good-will toward all the members of this Sisterhood, and that I will never willingly go to my rest at night without seeking reconciliation with any of them whom I may have offended, or who may have offended me.

"To all of which I bind myself, with a full intention and purpose of soul to keep and perform the same, the Lord being my helper, that I may be the handmaid of Christ, in the midst of an evil world; and in this mind I offer myself for communion in the Holy Sacrament of the Body and Blood of Christ, in testimony to my Lord, and to you, my Sisters, that I have chosen the Lord to serve Him."

¶ *Here shall follow a celebration of the Holy Communion, in which the whole Community shall, if possible, receive.*

RULE II.

The Probationers shall make the following pledge :

⁋ *The pledge of a Sister being read to the Candidate, she shall make answer and say:*

"I desire to make trial of my faith and love by doing as these Sisters do, and learning by their faith and love, with all fidelity of soul, under their counsel and guidance, for the space of—— ——. In the Name of the Father, and of the Son, and of the Holy Ghost. Amen."

⁋ *And each Probationer shall subscribe her name to the Sister's pledge, in witness of this her profession.*

RULE III.

The Superior, upon being inducted into office, shall make this pledge :

"I (A. B.), being duly appointed Superior of the Sisterhood of St. John, do promise and engage that I will be instant in prayer, that the power of Christ may rest upon me, and His grace enable me for my office. And I pray you, my Pastor, and you, my Sisters, lend me your aid, that I may keep this pledge unblemished and unimpaired, to the glory of Christ, and the benefit of this Community, and of the whole Sisterhood of St. John. In the Name of the Father, and of the Son, and of the Holy Ghost. Amen."

RULE IV.

Every Sister and every Probationer shall, as far as possible, have a specific duty assigned to her, for which she shall be responsible. Any complaint concerning the performance of that duty must be made to her. And only in case of alleged neglect of such complaint by her may it be carried to the Superior.

RULE V.

The Superior is bound to notice and reprove any neglect or deficiency in any department, directly with the Sister in charge of such department.

She shall not take action upon any complaint without notifying the Sister concerned; nor shall she address any censure or reproof to any Sister in the presence of any third person. But advice and orders concerning the discharge of duty shall never be taken as implying censure.

RULE VI.

Any Sister or Probationer may appeal from the

censure of the Superior to the Pastor ; but such appeal must be made at the first opportunity, with the least possible delay.

RULE VII.

In all censures, the Superior shall study gentleness, and the Sisters meekness; and each shall admonish the other to the observance of this rule.

RULE VIII.

No grievance or complaint shall be discussed by the Sisters and Probationers in conversation ; but every member of the Community shall diligently endeavor to conceal her knowledge of misunderstandings and difficulties.

RULE IX.

The Community shall observe three hours of prayer, besides the services in the Parish Church. The hours shall be fixed by the Superior, and shall only be changed in case of urgent necessity. But, in case of clashing between the hours of the Community and the hours of the Parish Church, the latter shall take precedence.

RULE X.

All the members of the Community who are not absolutely prevented by other duties, or by sickness, shall attend the services of the Sisterhood, in the private Oratory, and also the services in the Parish Church.

RULE XI.

The Pastor shall appoint the form of Prayer to be used in the Oratory, and also a short form to be used by those whose duties forbid their attendance at the Oratory, that all may unite in worship at the appointed hours.

RULE XII.

The Sisters and Probationers shall assemble in Chapter, every evening, immediately before the third hour of prayer, for mutual consultation and encouragement. Bnt no votes shall be taken at such meetings, except the said meeting shall have been duly warned as provided in the Statutes.

RULES OF THE ASSOCIATES.

1. ONE hour of every day shall be devoted unto the Lord, in the fellowship of the Sisterhood of St. John, and in the obedience of this Order. The same shall be observed day by day without intermission or interruption, except through sick-

ness or other controlling necessity, and hours thus lost shall be redeemed on days following, as rapidly as possible.

2. The Associate Superior shall assign and appoint to each Associate her duty and work for the consecrated hour, with due regard to the abilities and circumstances of each, and every Associate shall do that which is appointed her without murmuring or remonstrance.

3. The Associates, while engaged in the outdoor work of the Sisterhood, shall wear a plain garb, not uniform and not singular.

4. The Associates shall pay no dues or fines of any sort for the maintenance of their Order or the furtherance of its work. But all contributions to the Order shall be offered, without name, at the Offertory in the Holy Communion.

5. Any Associate who earns her bread by daily labor may, at her own request, be assigned to duty in her regular vocation for the benefit of the Order, she consecrating one twenty-fourth part of her daily earnings to the common fund of the Order.

6. The Associate Superior shall have the custody of the common fund of the Order, and

shall administer the same at her sole discretion, accounting therefor monthly to the Pastor.

7. The common fund shall consist of all offerings of the Associates and of others, offered as specified in Rule 4, and of all the earnings of the Associates during the consecrated hour.

8. The Associate Superior shall never make known to any person whatsoever, except to the Pastor, the amount contributed by any donor to the objects of the Order.

9. The Associates shall earnestly cultivate peace, love, and good-will, one towards another, and never wilfully suffer a misunderstanding or difference to go unreconciled, so that the sun should go down upon their wrath.

10. Any Associate who has no work assigned her, may select her own work for the day, or may devote the hour for that day to special acts and exercises of devotion in behalf of the Order, and the whole Sisterhood, either in public or private worship.

9.
Deaconesses' Association of the Diocese of Long Island.

THE following extract from the annual Address of the Rt. Rev. A. N. Littlejohn, D.D., Bishop of Long Island, at the Convention of that Diocese held in 1872, will explain the origin of the body of Deaconesses at present engaged in the service of the Church in Brooklyn, N. Y.

DEACONESSES.

"At our last Convention, I called attention somewhat at length to the importance of early action upon the subject of "The Organized Work of Christian Women" in this Diocese. The Convention promptly seconded my recommendation and appointed a Special Committee to consider and report upon it to this Convention. Meanwhile, there has been a remarkable and unlooked for advance in the feeling and opinion of the whole Church in regard to this matter. It assumed a very prominent place among the topics discussed at the late General Convention by the Board of

Missions then assembled. It was also warmly advocated in the Pastoral Letter of the House of Bishops. So far as could be discovered, it received the cordial and unanimous approval of all the members of the General Convention and of the Board of Missions. So far as the sentiment of the Church was concerned, I felt that there was no longer any reason for delaying action in this Diocese. Evidently the time had come to translate feeling into practice and opinion into fact. With the full assurance, therefore, of the active sympathy and public endorsement of this Convention, and of every member of our Diocese, I availed myself of the earliest opportunity afforded me to carry the mind of the Church into effect. Accordingly, on Quinquagesima Sunday, February 11, in St. Mary's Church, Brooklyn, I publicly admitted six godly and well-tried women to the office of Deaconess; and on the evening of the 15th of March, in Emmanuel Church, Brooklyn, one—in all seven. Of these, two are employed in the Church Charity Foundation; (one having been appointed Deaconess in charge of all the Branches of the Foundation); one has charge of our Mission in the Public Institutions of the County, in Flatbush ; and four are engaged in Parish work. The labors of these trained and authorized women have already been richly blessed. The work they are doing to-day sufficiently vindicates the wisdom of the action which has been taken. Their presence in our Houses of Mercy and in our Hospitals is a power already thankfully recognized. It will introduce into their management the order, efficiency and loving spirit, without which such Institutions, however liberal their support and ample their means of doing good, attain only half their influence and usefulness. As their numbers increase and their discipline is perfected, these skilled and devoted women will be ready to respond to the calls of sickness, death and affliction in our private homes, coming to us not only as messengers of mercy, but as trained and experienced helpers for Christ's sake in the days of our sorrow and trial.

"The Parish Clergy, who have welcomed them to their side as fellow-workers among the poor, the fallen, and the suffering of every name, bear grateful testimony to the value of their unobtrusive, obedient and systematic service."

DEACONESSES OF THE DIOCESE OF LONG ISLAND.

DEFINITION.—*A Deaconess is a woman set apart by a Bishop, under that title, for service in the Church.*

GENERAL PRINCIPLES.

1. No Deaconess shall officially accept or resign work in this Diocese without the express authority of the Bishop, which authority may at any time be withdrawn.

2. A Deaconess shall be free to resign her commission as Deaconess after six months' notice to the Bishop, or she may be deprived of it at any time by the Bishop.

3. A Deaconess, if engaged in a parish, shall work under the direction and supervision of the Incumbent of that parish, and shall report through him to the Bishop every three months. If engaged in any organized charity, or in any mission of the Diocese, she shall work under the direction and supervision of the Bishop, or of such clergyman as the Bishop may appoint, and shall report once in three months to the Bishop.

4. In every parish, or mission, or organized charity of the Diocese employing a Deaconess, there shall be, if possible, Associates, who may

At Home and Abroad.

assist in the following ways, and in others, if required :

(1.) To collect alms.

(2.) To procure work for the poor, and to promote its sale.

(3.) To teach in the Sunday or Parochial Schools.

(4.) To help in the music or others classes.

(5.) To relieve the destitute and minister to the sick.

(6.) To aid the Pastor in bringing forward and preparing candidates for the Holy Baptism and Confirmation.

(7.) To attend to funeral arrangements for the poor.

5. Associates shall be appointed and removed by the Bishop. If to be engaged in parish-work, they must be nominated by the Rector or Minister under whom they are to labor.

RULES.

1. As it is needful that no one be admitted to the office of Deaconess without careful previous preparation, both technical and religious, every one who shall have received the Bishop's consent

to her becoming a candidate for the diaconate shall serve at least six months as a probationer.

2. No one shall be admitted as Deaconess without giving proper assurance of her intention to continue in this office for the space of three years at least.

3. The Deaconess shall maintain her habit of prayer and meditation, and shall aim at continual progress in Christian knowledge and life. To this end there shall be stated meetings for joint acts of prayer and worship, and, as often may be, for the joint reception of the Holy Communion.

4. The dress of the Deaconess shall be uniform, simple, and distinctive.

5. The ordinary official designation of a Deaconess shall be Sister A—— or B—— (using the Christian name). The official signature shall be (full Christian and surname) "A—— B——, Deaconess."

THE FORM OF ADMITTING DEACONESSES TO THEIR OFFICE,

ACCORDING TO THE USE OF THE DIOCESE OF LONG ISLAND.

¶ *To the congregation, all standing:*

DEARLY BELOVED IN THE LORD:

We are met together in the fear of God, and trusting in His Holy Name, to receive and to ratify the pledge of obedient and loving service offered by these our Sisters, here present; and, under the invocation of the blessed Name of Him whom they desire to serve, to admit them to the office of Deaconess in the Church of God.

In their several places they purpose to serve their heavenly Lord and Master Jesus Christ in the persons of His poor and sick and suffering members. For His sake they seek the privilege of living only to serve the widow and the orphan, the sick and the destitute, the wretched and the distressed. Under His blessing, and by the constituted authority of His Church, they desire to follow those holy women who of old ministered to the Lord in person, and those whom His Apostles admitted to be helpers in the work, and succorers of themselves and others.

They are of "good report," as was required of those first admitted to serve tables in the Church. They have been diligent in prayer for the Holy Spirit, and for the wisdom which is from above. They hold, as we are persuaded, the mystery of the faith in a pure conscience. In outward walk and conversation they have been found sober and faithful. Their skilfulness and devotion in the service of the sick and poor, their docility and orderly obedience to those set over them in the Lord, have been duly tried.

Dear Sisters in the Lord:

We exhort you in the Name of our Lord Jesus Christ that you have constantly in your remembrance into how high a dignity and charge you are called; even to be helpers of those who are messengers and watchmen and stewards of the Lord; and to see that you never cease from your labors, care, and diligence, until you have done all that in you lieth, according to your bounden duty, to lift up the fallen, to instruct the ignorant, to comfort the weary and heavy laden; and to bring them that are without into the fold of Christ.

But forasmuch as this office is of so great difficulty, you see how watchfully and earnestly you ought to apply yourselves thereto, that you may fulfil the same and give no occasion to the enemy to speak reproachfully. Howbeit you cannot have a mind and will thereto of yourselves; for these are of God alone. You have need, therefore, to pray unceasingly for His Holy Spirit, to be diligent in the reading of the Holy Scriptures, to be well instructed in the ways of His Church, so that you may become, in word and deed, patterns of all womanly and Christian virtues. We are assured that you have already, by God's grace, determined to give yourselves wholly to the service of the Lord, and especially to that office to which you have been called, and that, forsaking all worldly cares and studies, you will (so long as God shall call you to this office) apply yourselves, as far as may be, to this one thing. May you be enriched with all spiritual gifts in Christ Jesus, and through them may you wax riper and stronger in your office, and daily grow more and more into the likeness of those blessed daughters of the Church who labored much in the Lord.

¶ *Then shall the Bishop say:*

The Lord be with you.

¶ *The people kneel.*

OUR FATHER, &C.

Bishop. Direct us, O Lord, in all our doings with Thy most gracious favor, and further us with Thy continual help, that in all our works, begun, continued, and ended in Thee, we may glorify Thy Holy Name, and finally, by Thy mercy, obtain everlasting life, through Jesus Christ our Lord. *Amen.*

Lord, we pray Thee that Thy grace may always prevent and follow us, and make us continually to be given to all good works; through Jesus Christ our Lord. *Amen.*—(*Collect for Seventh Sunday after Trinity.*)

Almighty and everlasting God, by whose Spirit the whole body of the Church is governed and sanctified; receive our supplications and prayers, which we offer before Thee for all estates of men in Thy holy Church, that every member of the same, in his vocation and ministry, may truly and godly serve Thee; through our Lord and Saviour Jesus Christ. *Amen.*—(*Second Collect for Good Friday.*)

O Almighty God, Who didst call Phœbe and Dorcas, and other holy women to be servants of Thy Church, and didst enable them to succour Thine Apostles, and others also; behold these Thy servants who have given themselves to a like ministration. So replenish them with all Christian graces, and adorn them with innocency of life, that, by their labors and good examples, they may faithfully serve Thee, to the glory of Thy Name, and the benefit of Thy holy Church; through Jesus Christ our Lord. *Amen.*

O Lord our heavenly Father, we beseech Thee mercifully to receive our prayers on behalf of these Thy servants. Make them to be modest, humble, and constant in their ministrations, that they may always have the testimony of a good conscience. Grant unto them, we pray Thee, such measures of Thy grace as they may from time to time need, that they may both perceive and know what things they ought to do, and also may have grace and power faithfully to fulfil the same; through Jesus Christ our Lord. *Amen.*

¶ *Then shall the Priest appointed thereto present unto the Bishop the persons to be admitted to the Office of Deaconess, saying:*

Reverend Father in God, I present unto you these persons to be admitted Deaconesses.

Bishop. Have the persons whom you present unto us been found meet, both for skill in womanly ministrations, and for godly life and conversation, to exercise this office?

Answer. I think them so to be.

¶ *Then shall the Bishop say:*

It is the duty of a Deaconess to minister to the poor, the sick, and the ignorant, and in all humility and godly submission, setting aside all unwomanly usurpation of authority in the Church, to help the ministers of God's Word and Sacraments.

Will you do this diligently and lovingly?

Answer. I will, by the help of God.

Bishop. Will you be obedient to them who are set over you in the Lord, cheerfully and faithfully performing the service that shall be appointed to you?

Answer. I will, by the help of God.

Bishop. Inasmuch as this Office is not to be lightly undertaken or relinquished, is it your present purpose to continue in it for the space of three years, at the least?

Answer. I purpose to do so, by the help of God.

Bishop. Inasmuch as you desire to be admitted to the office of Deaconess, will you faithfully observe such rules as the Bishop may prescribe; and be ready to give yourself willingly and thoroughly to any work which may be appointed to you, as long as you remain in this office?

Answer. I will do so, by the help of God.

Bishop. Almighty God, Who has called you to serve Him in this holy life, give you the power to fulfil this your service acceptably, through Jesus Christ our Lord. *Amen.*

¶ *Then shall the Bishop, taking each candidate by the right hand, give her his blessing:*

God the Father, God the Son, and God the Holy Ghost bless, preserve, and sanctify thee: and so fill thee with all faith, wisdom, charity and humility, that thou mayest serve before Him, to the glory of His great Name and the benefit of His holy Church, and in the end attain to everlasting life, through the merits and mediation of our Lord and Saviour Jesus Christ. *Amen.*

I admit thee, dearly beloved, to the office of

Deaconess, in the Name of the Father, and of the Son, and of the Holy Ghost. *Amen.*

¶ *After which, all kneeling:*

Bishop. Our help is in the Name of the Lord.

Answer. Who hath made heaven and earth.

Bishop. O Lord, bless Thine handmaidens.

Answer. And let them find grace in Thy sight.

Bishop. Make them a clean heart, O Lord.

Answer. And renew a right spirit within them.

Bishop. Give them fulness of joy in Thy presence.

Answer. And the peace which passeth all understanding.

Bishop. Give Thine angels charge over them.

Answer. That the enemy may not approach to hurt them.

Bishop. Keep them in the way of Thy commandments.

Answer. That they may persevere unto the end and be saved.

Bishop. O Lord, hear our prayer.

Answer. And let our cry come unto Thee.

Bishop. Eternal God, Father of our Lord Jesus Christ, Creator both of man and woman, Who didst replenish Miriam and Deborah and Anna and Huldah with Thy Spirit, Who didst not disdain that Thy only begotten Son should be born of a woman; look now Thyself on these Thine handmaidens here set apart for the office of Deaconess; give unto them Thy Holy Spirit, cleanse them from all filthiness of flesh and spirit, that they may worthily accomplish the work now committed unto them, to the glory of Thy Name, through Jesus Christ our Lord. *Amen.*

Bishop. The peace of God, &c.

HYMN.

How blessed, from the bonds of care
   And earthly fetters free,
In singleness of heart and aim,
   Thy servants, Lord, to be!
The hardest toil to undertake,
   With joy at Thy command,
The meanest office to receive
   With meekness, at Thy hand!

With willing heart and longing eyes,
   To watch before Thy gate,
Ready to run the weary race,
   To bear the heavy weight;
No voice of thunder to expect,
   But follow calm and still,
For love can easily divine
   The One Beloved's will.

Thus may we serve Thee, gracious Lord!
　Thus ever Thine alone,
Our souls and bodies given to Thee,
　The purchase Thou hast won.
Through evil or through good report,
　Still keeping by Thy side,
By life or death, in this poor flesh
　Let Christ be magnified!

How happily the working days
　In this dear service fly!
How rapidly the closing hour,
　The time of rest draws nigh!
When all the faithful gather home,
　A joyful company;
And ever where the Master is,
　Shall His own servants be.
Amen.

PART SECOND.

V.
SISTERHOODS AND DEACONESSES ABROAD.

THE organization of women into associations for Christian service in the Church of England and among the Reformed communions of the continent of Europe, dates back nearly a quarter of a century. In Germany and France, where these associations are very numerous, the Christian women, organized under their Rules, have ordinarily borne the name of Deaconesses; while in the Church of England, though there are Associations of Deaconesses, as in London and Liverpool, organizations of women have thus far more generally taken the form of Sisterhoods. The following pages contain a brief account of some of the better known of these Associations in England and on the continent. They are chosen from among many others, simply because they may be accepted as types of the various Institutions abroad, in which godly women, widely differing often in their personal views, but actuated by a common desire to dedicate themselves to the service of Christ, have been successfully associated.

It is not generally known that beside the Institutions organized at Kaiserswerth, in Prussia, there are many others scattered in France, Switzerland, Germany, and Sweden, all of which follow, more or less closely, the model furnished in the admirable organization of Fliedner. Among these, that organized by the French Evangelical Communion in Paris, in 1842, that begun at Echallens in Switzerland, in 1843,(now removed to St. Loup near Lausanne,) and those at Zurich, Strasburg, Utrecht, and in Sweden, have been signally useful and successful.

In England there are, at present, between thirty and forty Sisterhoods, the more prominent of which are the Sisterhood of St. John the Baptist, at Clewer, (an account of which will be found in the following pages,) and the Sisterhood of St. Margaret, at East Grinstead. There are branch houses of this latter Sisterhood at London, Aberdeen, Wigan, and Frome-Selwood, where day and night schools, guilds, and other useful works of charity are conducted by the Sisters.

As already intimated, organizations of Deaconesses in the Church of England have been thus far less numerous than the societies known as Sisterhoods. There are, however, vigorous and successful associations of Deaconesses in London, Salisbury, Chester, Ely, Bedford and Liverpool. An account of the Mildmay Deaconesses' Home will be found included in this volume.

1.
House of Mercy.

CLEWER, ENGLAND.*

FOUNDED A.D. 1849.

Visitor: THE LORD BISHOP OF OXFORD.
Warden: THE REV. T. T. CARTER, M.A.

THIS House is the parent House of the Sisterhood of St John Baptist, under whose care the various works mentioned below, in addition to the Penitentiary, are being carried on. The House is able to accommodate about eighty penitents.

Besides the full Sisters, a second Order was formed, A.D. 1860, of ladies unable to devote themselves wholly to community life, constrained to limit their residence in the house or one of its branch establishments to a certain number of months in the year. They live under the same rule as the regular Sisters while resident with

---

* The account of Clewer herewith given, is compiled from (a) *The Kalender of the Church of England;* (b) *An Essay on Sisterhoods,* by Mrs. Sarah B. Wister, together with other unpublished sources of information.

them; but, when absent, they are free to conform themselves to the habits of their own homes. They form their engagements for three years, to be renewed if desired.

Associates.—These are ladies living in their own homes, and giving such assistance to the work as their circumstances may permit. Their engagements consist (*a*) in offering up prayer on behalf of the House of Mercy; (*b*) in undertaking some charge—as, *e.g.*, to collect alms, provide employment for the penitents, assist in the sale of their work, or find situations in service for those who may be recommended. The Associates are remembered in the prayers of the Community. There are also male Associates under the same rule, who are bound to different kinds of charitable works, suited to their state.

The works described below do not constitute any charge upon the funds of the House of Mercy. They are sustained by means entirely distinct, for which others, who are immediately concerned with them are responsible.

ST. JOHN'S ORPHANAGE, CLEWER.

COMMENCED A.D. 1854.

This House has accommodation for twenty-five orphan children and twenty industrial girls training for service. The orphans and industrial girls are children, not of the fallen, but of respectable parents. *Terms*—Children under 14 years of age, 12*l.* per annum; the industrial class and those training for teachers, 10*l.* per annum. The sum of 3*l.* is also required with each child when admitted to provide her with clothing according to the school regulations.

ST. ANDREW'S CONVALESCENT HOSPITAL, CLEWER.

FOR INVALIDS OF BOTH SEXES.

This Hospital is built to accommodate sixty patients (twenty-four men, twenty women, and sixteen children). Funds are needed to clear the debt on the building account. *Terms*—8*s.* a-week.

ST. ANDREW'S COTTAGE, CLEWER.

The Home has accommodation for nine ladies, either recovering from sickness and requiring

AT HOME AND ABROAD. 277

change of air and nourishing food, or those needing rest from over-fatigue or sorrow. No one is eligible who is or who has suffered from contagious or mental disease, or who is not sufficiently convalescent to be able to join the family at dinner. The time of their stay varies from one week to six weeks. The terms (payable weekly in advance) are 10*s*. a-week in the doubled-bedded rooms, which are divided by curtains, 14*s*. in single rooms, and there is one room at 1*l*. These payments include household medicine, and everything except wine, washing, and bed-room fires.

ST. STEPHEN'S MISSION, CLEWER.

This Mission was opened in the year 1867. The buildings consist of school-rooms and class-rooms, and accommodation for Sisters and others working with or under them. The chancel of the Church is now built and opened for Service.

In addition to the above the Sisterhood conducts a school for the children of clergymen and professional men residing abroad, which is known as St. John's School, Pimlico ; an Orphanage, also in Pimlico, and St. John the Baptist Mission in Soho, to which is attached a chaplain. Besides the above they have under their care the following institutions : In

BOVEY TRACY.
THE HOUSE OE MERCY FOR THE COUNTY OF DEVON.
Established a.d. 1861.

This House is now completed, and capable of receiving, if funds can be supplied, seventy-two inmates. There are now fifty-eight, the present funds not sufficing for the reception of more.

IN OXFORD.
FEMALE PENITENTIARY AND HOUSE OF REFUGE.

Visitor: The Lord Bishop of Oxford.
President: The Ven. C. C. Clerke, Archdeacon of Oxford.
Secretary: The Rev. W. J. Tait, Worcester College.

This Society consists of the Visitor, President, Secretary, Chaplain, a Committee composed of nine clergymen and nine laymen, together with the two Proctors of the University. The personal care of the penitents is in the hands of the

Sisters of St. John the Baptist, working under the guidance of the Chaplain.

There is a laundry and sewing-room in the House, which are very beneficial to the Institution, as they supply employment and opportunities of instruction in useful work, whilst the profits of the laundry are by no means inconsiderable.

IN TORQUAY,
ST. RAPHAEL'S CONVALESCENT HOME.

Warden: THE REV. THE HON. C. L. COURTENAY.

This Home is for women of good character recovering from illness, and also for delicate persons from any part of England, not incurably ill, but needing sea air, medical care, and good nursing. 5s. to 8s. weekly, or 30s. monthly, to be paid in advance with each patient.

It is now desired to add a chapel, and to enlarge the building, so that nurses may be received for training, and that it may be possible to retain a *few* cases in which convalescence has become hopeless.

The "SOHO HOUSE OF CHARITY" is also under the charge of the same Sisterhood.

The following account of the Sisterhood of St. John Baptist, is from the pen of a recent American visitor,* and is the more valuable, because it is, certainly, the account of one influenced by no prejudice in favor of the Order :

"Among the numerous communities of women in England, that of Clewer has been longest established, and is universally spoken of as the most successful example of an Anglican Sisterhood : great praise is given to its hospitals and the nursing of its Sisters, even by those who do not think well of the mode of life. To Clewer, accordingly, I went, without prejudice or prepossession, and entirely unprepared for the sort of thing I found. The railway station is at Windsor, and as I was inquiring the way of a porter, a figure in the dress of a nun passed me, walking with the peculiar step, which every one who comes to Europe soon learns to recognize as the conventual gait. I say, in general terms, 'the dress of a nun,' for it was black and clinging ; there was a deep cape, a long veil, a white cap, and a crucifix : there may have been special buttons which distinguished it from a nun's dress, but that was the effect. 'There goes one of the Sisters,' said the porter. I ran after her and asked her if she would show me the way to Clewer. She turned a sweet, fresh, intelligent young face upon me, and in a still sweeter voice assented. We walked along the dusty road together for about a mile. The autumn sun was shining with unusual brightness for England, but it was still early in the day, and the air was chilly. I noticed that my companion's hands—a lady's hands—were gloveless, and red and purple from cold. Windsor straggles out on one side in detached houses and cottages until it reaches the ugly and unpromising village of Clewer. Here my guide, who had been talking busily about the institution, stopped and said that there was a

* Mrs. S. B. Wister.

mission-school, if I would like to see it. It was a low, gabled building, with some architectural pretension. As we turned in at the gate she was greeted eagerly by a group of children in the street. She spoke to them by name, and asked why they were not at school. They gave their excuse, and the eldest girl, looking at her with beaming eyes, exclaimed, 'Oh, Sister, wont you go and see Agnes soon ? She *do* want to see you so !' The Sister smiled, blushed a little, looked down, and explained carelessly that 'Agnes' was a sick child ; but the little scene spoke for itself.

"The school is a very well arranged building, sunny, clean, and airy : the aspect of all the rooms was bright and wholesome. There are rooms for children of every age, also of every condition, for after attempting to classify them only according to years or learning, it has been found necessary to separate them according to their station in life—a troublesome and complicated division, but answering much better than the other. This does not include the first two rooms, one a mere *crèche*, where toddling things of two years old and under are kept out of mischief, nor the infant school ; and naturally these comprise only children of the lower orders. Above these grades there are three distinct sets of classes, arranged according to the age, station, and advancement of the pupils : and after a certain period the girls and boys are separate. All these are taught by members of the institution. Some of the children are inmates of the house, especially older girls, who are being educated as governesses : some of these were taking music-lessons. Every possible advantage is given them. All the children looked clean and tidy, even those who were almost in rags. My Sister said that cleanliness is made a *sine qua non* with the parents ; the rooms were all perfectly fresh and sweet; the children looked happy, the teachers very happy.

"We left the school, and went on beyond the thickly-built part of the village to where the houses stood sparsely again, and presently came in sight of a group of handsome buildings with a peculiar ecclesiastical stamp, difficult to define, but impossible to mistake. These were the hospital, for sixty patients; the home for indigent ladies, with accommodation for nine; the orphan asylum, for fifty; and the house of mercy, which will contain eighty 'Penitents,' besides the Sisters. The scale of the work took me altogether by surprise. In addition to these there are several branch establishments—a school, an orphanage, a mission, and a house of charity in London, a house of mercy and hospital in different parts of Devonshire, a female penitentiary at Oxford, and a sanatorium and schools at Folkestone. At the hospital my gentle guide left me, and I was consigned to another Sister, a very striking person, with a remarkable expression of power and restrained will in her face. My interest in her was heightened by my knowledge that she was a fellow-countrywoman, and that, though not much above thirty, she had been placed at the head of a cholera hospital in London at the last outbreak. She showed me all over the hospital, discoursing quietly but steadily the while about the institution. I never saw so beautiful a hospital: its order and convenience reminded me of some of our military hospitals during the war. The brightness and taste of its arrangements were like those of a special sick-room: these were effected by a few flowers, engravings, and gay-colored table and bed-covers, which, without in the least detracting from the air of cleanliness—the first requisite in a sick-room—went far to modify the ordinary hospital look, which is not cheerful. Kitchens, refectories, wards, offices, all wore the same neat, orderly, home-like aspect, and the halls and staircases are very handsome, and of fine, large proportions. Every building of the establishment is planned with due regard to future additions. All the nurses and attendants wear the dress of the Sisterhood.

"We then went to the house of mercy, the mother-house of the society. Its object is to reclaim fallen women, who after a certain residence, are successively called penitents and Magdalens—the latter only after having made a 'profession' and received 'consecration:' Sisters they never can become. Here again, the utmost order and neatness reigned, and the desire for embellishment was visible in many engravings, photographs, illuminated mottoes and monograms, which were all of a religious character, and scarcely softened the monastic simplicity and severity of the household arrangements. The kitchen, laundries, refectories, dormitories, and private apartments of the Sisters—which are separate from those of their unfortunate inmates—were samples of system and order. The chapel is very rich: they have succeeded in producing an illusory effect of the real thing; it is a complete specimen, too, of the extreme complexity which pervades the whole establishment. There is a seat for the Mother Superior, higher than the rest; there are separate places for the postulants, the novices, the full Sisters, the penitents, the Magdalens; a gallery, almost closed, for strangers, and another closely latticed, for—most sad to say—*lady penitents*, women of good position, who are mercifully allowed a greater share of seclusion when they seek refuge and a place for repentance here.

"I had no time to visit the orphanage or the home for invalid ladies, but from their external aspect there could be no doubt that the same order, propriety, taste, and wonderful administrative power were paramount here. Among the branch institutions are schools for training girls for service; missions for district-visiting among the poor and sick; convalescent homes for needy women of good character who require rest and change of air; boarding-schools for young ladies; *a night-school for tramps*, in the worst part of Windsor.

"'How do you approach such people?' I exclaimed. 'How can you hope to get the smallest hold upon them?'

"'I hardly know,' was the reply; 'they come to the school the night or two that they stop in the place, they seem pleased that we feel interest enough in them to try and collect them, and they often leave their children with us when they go off.' Verily this is spiritual bread cast upon the waters.

"The Sisterhood is that of St. John the Baptist. There are two orders of Sisters, the first order consisting of two classes: the postulancy lasts six months, the novitiate two years for the first class, four years for the second class; after which the member is in full fellowship and called a Confirmed Sister. The second order consists of those unable to live entirely in the community: while doing so they are subject to the same rules as the other Sisters; when in their own homes they are merely expected, as far as possible, to conform their dress and mode of life to their special profession. There are also Sister Associates—single women not belonging to the community, or members of either of the other orders, who devote themselves to live by the same rule as far as possible. Besides these are the Associates—ladies living in their own homes and aiding the Sisterhood by prayer, collecting arms, finding places for the penitents and girls of the industrial schools, etc. No one is admitted as a Sister unless a member of the Church of England, or, if under thirty, without the consent of her parents. Each Sister who is able is expected to contribute at least fifty pounds (two hundred and fifty dollars) per annum toward the maintenance of the house. The vows are taken for life—obedience, poverty, and chastity. They are scrupulous to spend as little money as possible: they travel third-class, and never call a hackney-coach when it can be avoided. This, no doubt, was also the secret of the ungloved hands on the cold morning. Their obedience is implicit and unquestioning. Although generally assigned to the work for which they have been found most fit—teaching, nursing, visiting the poor, influencing the penitents, or exercising any special talent for the use of the community—they may be sent anywhither without a moment's warning by the Mother Superior, and without any idea when they may be recalled.

"The Sisters have entire freedom to correspond with, and receive visits from, their friends. There are also vacations—more properly leaves of absence—at stated times, and for a stated length of time, when they may go to them."

The following extracts from the Statutes of the Clewer *House of Mercy*, will throw further light upon the government of the Sisterhood of St. John the Baptist, and its relation to that Institution :

The object of the Institution, called the Clewer House of Mercy, is the reception and protection of women who have led unchaste lives, with a view, by means of such reception and protection, to their reformation and ultimate safe establishment, either in some reputable calling by which to earn a livelihood, or otherwise ; and such Institution shall consist of a Visitor, a Warden, a Superior, Sisters, a Council, Trustees, and two Treasurers.

The Bishop for the time being of the Diocese in which the said Institution is situated, shall be the Visitor, if he will accept that Office ; but if he shall refuse, then the Council shall elect such person as they shall think fit, until there shall be a new Bishop of the same Diocese, when the Office shall be offered by the Council to such new Bishop ; and so, from time to time, such Bishop for the time being of the said Diocese, or, in case of his refusal, the person so elected by the Council as aforesaid, shall be the Visitor for the time being. And such Visitor shall have full power and authority, as well upon his own mere motion as upon appeal lodged, or complaint made, to do and order all those things which appertain by law to the office of Visitor, or which shall be hereinafter specially provided.

The Warden shall be a Clergyman of the Church of England in priest's orders.

The Warden shall be appointed by the Council ; but if, on the occasion of any vacancy, the Council shall not appoint a new Warden before the expiration of six calendar months next after the term at which such vacancy shall have happened, then the appointment shall lapse to the Visitor.

The Warden shall not be removable from his office, except by a vote of at least three-fourths of such members of the Council as shall be present at a meeting specially convened for the purpose of taking into consideration the propriety of such removal.

The Warden shall perform, or be responsible for the due performance of, the religious services, and superintend the teaching and spiritual discipline of the inmates.

The Warden shall have power, with the approval of the Council, from time to time to appoint a Sub-Warden, who shall assist him in the performance of such of his duties as he may assign to him, and such Sub-Warden shall, during every vacancy in the office of Warden, perform the duties thereof.

The Sub-Warden shall be a Clergyman of the Church of England in priest's orders.

The Warden and Sub-Warden, to qualify them for their offices, must obtain the license of the Bishop of the Diocese, and be subject to his authority as other Clergymen officiating under his license.

The Sub-Warden may be dismissed by the Warden, or by a vote of at least three-fourths of such Members of the Council as shall be present at a meeting specially convened for the purpose of considering the propriety of such dismissal.

The Superior shall be a fully-admitted Sister, and shall be appointed in manner hereinafter mentioned, and shall (subject to the superintendence of the Warden) have the Government of the Sisters and other inmates of the said Institution, and of the household thereof.

On every vacancy of the office of Superior, the Warden shall nominate in writing to the fully-admitted Sisters a successor ; and if they shall, by a majority of votes, approve of the person so nominated, such person shall then succeed to the office ; but if such nomination shall not be so approved within twenty-one days, then the Warden shall in like manner nominate another person for approval, and if such second nomination be not approved of within one calendar month from the communication thereof to the Sisters, then the appointment shall lapse to the Visitor.

The Superior shall continue in office for the period of three years, but may at the end of that period be re-appointed.

The Superior may be removed by the Visitor on complaint

of the Council or Warden, but the Warden shall not lay such complaint before the Visitor until it shall have been previously submitted at, and considered by, the Council.

The Warden and Superior may from time to time appoint any fully-admitted Sister to be Assistant Superior for such period as they shall think proper; and during any vacancy in the office of Superior, or during the absence or incapacity of the Superior by reason of illness, such Assistant shall perform the duties of that office. And if on any such vacancy, absence, or incapacity, there shall be no Assistant Superior, the senior Sister in order of admission shall act as Superior for the time being.

The Assistant Superior may be removed by the Warden and Superior.

The Sisters shall consist of two classes, Sisters fully admitted after probation, and Sisters Probationary, the term and nature of probation to be settled in the Regulations hereinafter mentioned; but the Warden and Superior (or the Warden alone, in case of a vacancy in the office of Superior) shall be at liberty to shorten the period of probation at his discretion in any particular case.

No person shall be admitted into the House as Sister Probationary unless a member of the Church of England, nor without the written consent of her parents if under the age of 30 years; such admission to be made by the Warden and Superior, except during a vacancy in the office of Superior, and then such admission may be by the Warden alone.

Every Sister shall have full and uncontrolled liberty, whenever she shall think fit, to leave the Institution.

Every Sister shall, upon admittance to probation, agree to be bound by and observe all the Statutes and Regulations of the Institution applicable to herself.

The Warden and Superior may, with the consent of the majority of the Sisters fully admitted, make and vary such Regulations for the internal management and discipline of the Sisters as shall be consistent with the Statutes of the Institution, and be approved of by the Visitor, and such **Regulations** shall be accessible to all Members of the Council.

Penitents shall be admitted or discharged by the Warden and Superior, provided that none shall be retained in the House for a longer period than two years without the consent of the Council.

The numbers of the Sisters and Penitents shall be determined from time to time by the Council.

The Council shall consist of nine clergymen, and nine laymen in full communion with the Church of England, together with the Warden, Sub-Warden (if any), and Treasurers; and except in cases specially provided, four members shall form a quorum.

Every vacancy in the Council shall be filled up by a majority of the Members present at a meeting thereof.

The expenditure of the Institution, and also the amount of all salaries or wages paid to any of the officers, or servants, or laborers thereof, shall be under the entire control and management of the Council, but the hiring of menial servants or laborers shall be by the Warden and Superior together.

The Council shall have power to appoint and remove a Secretary and other officers.

The Council shall have power to make and vary by-laws for the government of its own body, and of any Committee thereof.

All meetings of the Council shall commence and conclude with prayer, and at each meeting of the Council, or of any Committee thereof, the members present shall, before proceeding to transact any other business, elect a Chairman of that meeting, who shall have a second or casting vote in every case of an equality of votes of the members present thereat.

Neither the Council nor any member thereof, simply as such, shall have any power to interfere in the internal management, regulations, or discipline of the House. But if at any time it shall appear to any member that any proceedings in the House or of any inmate thereof ought to be inquired into, he may, by a requisition in writing, signed by himself and two other members of the Council, and stating the matter to be inquired into, require the Secretary to call a Special Meeting of the Council to take such matter into consideration, and the Secretary shall thereupon forthwith call such Special Meeting at some time, not being less than five days nor more than ten days from the day on which such requisition shall be delivered to him. And if it shall appear to a majority of the members assembled at such meeting, that the matter requires further investigation, their resolution shall forthwith be communicated to the Visitor, who shall be requested to inquire into the matter with all convenient speed, and to communicate his judgment thereon in writing to the Council.

2.
Mildmay Deaconesses' Home,
LONDON, ENGLAND.

THIS Institution was organized under the vicar of the parish in which it is situated, in the year 1860. It had been a project earnestly thought of by its founders for many years, but when at length their plans took form, it was upon a very modest scale. Since then the institution has grown, until between one hundred and fifty and two hundred women have entered the Home as candidates for various spheres of missionary labor, and are to-day scattered through England, Scotland and Ireland, and also in Syria, Africa, China and India.

The organization of the institution is characterized by great freedom and simplicity, and while in its general spirit it follows the system originated at Kaiserswerth ; its details are characterized by marked elasticity and a happy facility of adaptedness to the work to which the Mildway Deaconesses have addressed themselves.

The following sketch, compiled from a recent volume,* edited by Mrs. Bayley, the author of " Ragged Homes and How to Mend them," will give an idea of the aims and workings of the institution.

Says the writer :

"Let me give a description of the first day after my arrival. At half-past six o'clock a bell rang to awaken the household, when each one was expected to rise at once, and to be in the dining-room by a quarter to eight, when the bell again sounded for morning prayers. All assembled as one large family, being mindful of family regulations ; indeed, during the whole of my stay there, I was struck with the general attention to punctuality, and the aim of each member not to interfere with the ordinary arrangements of the day. Little groups quickly formed themselves, and I overheard some of the conversation, in which I could not fail to observe the thoughtful consideration and kindness of the Sisters to each other.

" In a few minutes the Lady Superintendent entered, and quietly took her seat at the head of the long dining-table, amid the general morning salutation. I had no doubt, from the moment I saw her, that she was beloved by every one there, and I soon found that she was truly a mother to them all. They not only looked up to her as the guide and director of the establishment, but also sought her constantly as a private friend and counsellor. All her plans, though very simple in their character, were orderly, methodical, and regular, and the Sisters seemed to take a pleasure in fulfilling her wishes, and doing all in their power to prove that the confidence placed in them was not misjudged.

" After the morning chapter had been read, she looked round

* "The Ministry of Woman." By A. T. L., with an introduction by Mrs. Bayley. London : S. W. Partridge & Co.

the room until her eye rested on one Sister, to whom she said, 'Will *you* pray this morning?' We all knelt down, and as the Sister prayed, my heart seemed drawn towards her. She pleaded simply and earnestly for a renewal of spiritual life; and I felt that she fully realized the necessity of constant communion with Christ, in order to lead an earnest, useful, and holy life.

"During breakfast, which seemed to be a good substantial meal, the Sisters carried on a great deal of conversation amongst themselves, which the Lady Superintendent at length interrupted, by asking each to repeat any text which might have been dwelling on her mind.

"After breakfast each one returned to her own room, and made her bed, during the quarter of an hour which elapsed before the morning Bible-class. This commences at nine o'clock, and on that morning the Vicar himself was present; but he sometimes sends one of his Curates, or the Lady Superintendent conducts it herself. At ten o'clock the Bibles were closed, and in a few minutes the room was left quite empty.

"I waited a while, listened to the active preparations which were being made on all sides, and wondering whether I should be allowed a share in the day's work.

"Presently one of the elder Sisters entered the room and said:

"'Will you pardon what may seem an apparent neglect of you for a little while, as this is a particularly busy half-hour? Some of our workers are about to sally forth to spend the day in their different districts, and to hold their regular classes and mothers' meetings. As some of the work carried on from this Home lies at a great distance, we have to see to their wants before they start; and those who are not going to what we call our 'out-lying missions' are preparing to spend the morning in their home districts, or in the parochial schools.'

"She left me again, and I waited about half an hour before her return.

"'Now,' she said, 'I believe the house is empty, or very nearly so.'

"'How is it that you are at home?' I asked; 'I trust it is not on my account, for I should be very sorry to hinder your work in any way.'

"'No,' she said, 'that is not the reason, I can tell you for your comfort. I have to attend to some home duties this morning. Besides, dear Miss ——,' she added, 'the Lady Superintendent always looks to one of her elder ones to care for the visitors, or for any new inmates; for as there are seldom less than twenty of us and sometimes more, it is not a very agreeable thing to be left alone, as we must be till thoroughly acquainted with the Sisters and the work which is going on. The fact is, we are all so fully engaged with our own or each other's work, that strangers would pass almost unnoticed, unless there were some one appointed to look after them.'

"'And have you been here long?' I asked.

"'Nearly five years, I think.'

"'And you have never repented the step you then took?'

"'How do you mean?' she answered. 'You know we are bound by no vows: one great advantage of this Home is its perfect freedom. You can be an inmate for as long or as short a time as you please. Some ladies, whose home-ties prevent their giving up much time to out-door labor, come here for a month or two in the year, in order to be able to devote a small portion of their time to systematic work for the Lord; but there are others who, like me, seem to have nothing to hinder them from choosing this as their life-work. But may it not be,' she said, speaking less rapidly, 'that the Master calls some of us to bear the burden and heat of active work throughout our whole lives, while others are called to the different, but not less honored, position of fulfilling their mission in passive work for Him?'

"'I quite think so,' I answered.

"'And now,' she continued, 'will you come with me to the invalid-kitchen? We will have to go through this house into the next, and down into the basement, which I must open at eleven o'clock, in order to supply some fifty dinners to the sick in the district.'

"We went together, and found a servant and one of the younger Deaconesses busily engaged in cooking. From eleven to one o'clock, tickets were brought which had been given by the Sisters or district-visitors to those who needed nourishment or little delicacies, as well as medical aid.

"Some received meat or broth, others puddings or jellies, as the case might require ; and thus into many a humble home went a supply of suitable nourishment for those who were not able to touch their ordinary food, and who had not the means of preparing those delicacies which their health required.

"The Sister who accompanied me devoted herself to talking to the women and children who came for their dinners, speaking a word of comfort and encouragement to each one, and making particular inquiries for the health of the sick one ; and I am sure she was well repaid for her ministry to them by the way in which their faces brightened up as they received the food from her hands, and listened to her words.

"I asked her if she relieved only the sick, or if these dinners were also supplied to the many who were suffering from deep poverty that winter. She told me that this department was only for the sick, but that there was an Institution in the poorest part of the parish which served two purposes, being a resort for the working-classes, where they could obtain food at very moderate prices, and also a place at which persons suffering from the overwhelming distress into which thousands had been thrown that winter by want of employment could have their wants supplied by showing a ticket which had been paid for and given away by the benevolent public. This had proved a most invaluable mode of relief, and had been the means of saving many a family from the fearful death of starvation.

"I asked her whether the inmates of the Home seemed as willing to render their services in looking after the bodily wants of the poor as in attending to their spiritual need. She assured me that they were cared for equally.

"'Do you mean to say that the Sisters are not bound by any rule?'

" 'Indeed I do. After our morning Bible-class, we all go to the work given to us, being bound by nothing save punctuality. We are told, when we first come to the Home, that we are trusted to occupy our time to the best advantage; and I have never known this trust to be abused. And with regard to the question of numbers living together, I have found out what a blessing a large circle may be. For instance, as evening draws on, you will see some of the Sisters coming in, with tired and not over clean faces, looking, almost asking, for a word of sympathy and love; and then it is such a comfort to feel that we are not working alone.'

"The bell again sounded, and I found it was for lunch, which would be on the table for an hour, during which time the Sisters working in the neighborhood were expected to come in and take what they required, without waiting for one another. I think about a dozen were there that day; but all seemed anxious to return to their work, and the meal was taken in comparative silence.

"I was soon called away by a message from the Lady Superintendent, who wished to speak to me. She told me that she was going that afternoon to one of the outlying missions, and asked me to accompany her. I gladly agreed to do so, being anxious to gather all the information I could during my limited visit.

"After being in the train for about half an hour, we arrived at the station, which was at a little distance from the Mission. We then threaded our way through several narrow streets, until we came to a house, on which the words 'Mission-Room' were written, and here we found two of the Sisters busily engaged in a Mother's meeting.

"We all returned to the Home by half-past five o'clock, and I confess that I felt somewhat in the condition of those who come back weary and worn after the day's campaign. We dined at six o'clock, and a most happy social meal it was; but my heart was full that evening, and I hardly heard what was said around me.

"At half-past nine o'clock, the day was closed by family prayers, which were conducted by the Lady Superintendent. She gathered up the work of the day, and laid it all before God, like the Apostles of old, who 'went and told Jesus both what they had done and what they had taught.'

"And now I may perhaps say a few words respecting those who first opened the Institution, and their motives for so doing.

"It must be understood that, although the Lady Superintendent is completely the mistress of her household, yet the responsibility of the whole regulation and management of the Institution rests chiefly with the Pastor and his wife. I was pleased to find this to be the case ; for I had often noticed the disadvantages arising from the unlimited power of the Lady Superior in other Sisterhoods belonging to the Church of England.

"I found that all the arrangements of the Home, from its smallest household details to its largest field of outlying work, were intimately known and directed by the clergyman and his wife ; and the Lady Superintendent consults them about all her plans and any alterations she may think needful. She is thus relieved of a great amount of responsibility, and can give her attention more entirely to the individual characters and spiritual necessities of those over whom she has the charge."

In addition to the work thus described, the Deaconesses carry on Ragged Schools, Bible Classes, Girls' Night Schools, Cottage Readings, House Visitations, a Home for Old Men and Women, and other similar branches of distinctively mission work. Laboring among the most degraded classes of London, their free and flexible system has demonstrated its entire adaptedness to the often grave and trying emergencies which they have been called upon to meet.

3.
The Deaconesses of Kaiserswerth,
RHENISH PRUSSIA.

NO work professing to give even the most superficial view of the organized efforts of women in our day would be otherwise than grievously incomplete were it to leave unnoticed the remarkable work accomplished during the present century through the agency of a single man—Pastor Fliedner of Kaiserswerth. However widely existing organizations in our own and other Reformed Communions may have departed from the model to be found beneath the blue flag on the banks of the Rhine, the influence of that beautiful and inspiring example can never be adequately estimated.

In preparing an account of Kaiserswerth for these pages, it has been felt that no more apt or vivid description of the work and its founder could well be furnished than that which is already to be found in De Liefde's admirable volume, "The

Romance of Charity,"* which is, itself, simply an abridgment of the same author's larger work, "Six Months among the Charities of Europe." The following sketches of Fliedner and Kaiserswerth are mainly compiled from the first-named source.

"At the time when Dr. Fliedner began his work, the Protestant Church in Germany was not ripe for taking any steps towards employing an official female agency. From the prisons, the hospitals, and the abodes of misery, crime, and destitution, Fliedner heard an alarming cry for help, which male agents, however willing to go to the rescue, could not respond to. A wise man once laid down this rule : 'If a work must be done and nobody is inclined to do it, *I* must.' This work had to be done ; and there *was* nobody willing to do it, as it seemed. What then was left for a heart like Fliedner's, but to exclaim, '*I* must do it!'

"He resolved on trying to call forth a band of Christian women, willing to devote their lives to the rescue of the lost, to the nursing of the sufferers, to the training of the neglected. Nor was the idea such a novelty as German Protestants at first supposed it to be. Vincent de Paul had set the example two hundred years before, by founding his institution of Sisters of Charity in the Roman Catholic Church. And Mrs. Fry, whose celebrity had become European, gave proof that Protestant women did not need to go to Rome to learn the practice of Christian love. It was her example, indeed, which inspired Fliedner. She showed that a Christian woman, when fitly trained, is able to find access where the way is closed to men : that the gentle touch of her finger may smooth roughnesses where the pressure of a man's hand would fail.

* "The Romance of Charity," by John De Liefde. London : Alex. Strahan.

"Fliedner was a poor young Candidat of twenty-two, when in 1822 he took charge of the church at Kaiserswerth, which was one of the smallest and poorest parishes of the Prussian Church. He was scarcely settled in his new sphere when his congregation was thrown into utter poverty, and partly dispersed, by the failure of a manufacturing firm which employed nearly all its members. The presbytery offered the poor young minister another church, but he declined to leave his flock.

"This was the pivot upon which Fliedner's life turned. To be able to carry out his great work he had to see and to learn many things for which the small village of Kaiserswerth afforded no opportunity. He must be made acquainted with the wants of the suffering and neglected population of his country, and then learn the way to supply them. His church was in debt, and, owing to the above-mentioned catastrophe, his people were unable to pay it. He would make a tour of the province in which he resided, with a view of collecting money to make up the deficiency. On this journey he made the acquaintance of the leading men in the Church, and especially in the sphere of Christian philanthropy. Their conversation enabled him to cast a glance into the depths of misery which prevailed among the lower classes, in the prisons, and in the hospitals. He returned home to his flock with the glad intelligence that he was able to pay their most urgent debts. But fresh difficulties arose. It was quite absurd to expect that these poor people would be able to meet the annual expenditure of their church and school; so Fliedner resolved to try to collect an endowment for both, and this time he directed his steps to Holland and Great Britain.

"He set out on his travels in 1823, and he obtained money in abundance : but he carried back with him a greater treasure than even the gold of England or the silver of Holland ; and this was a thorough knowledge of the chief philanthropic and charitable institutions of the two countries. 'On my journey through those evangelical countries,' he wrote, some twenty years ago, 'I became acquainted with a great many institutions for the cure both of body and soul : schools and educational establishments, poorhouses, orphanages, and hospitals, Bible and missionary societies, etc. In August 1824 I returned home, full of admiration and gratitude, but at the same time ashamed that we Germans allowed ourselves thus to be excelled in works of Christian love, and especially that we had hitherto cared so little for our prisons.'

"It was precious seed which he brought home, and he failed not to sow it as soon as he could, and with all carefulness. 'The smallness of my church,' he wrote, 'allowed me more leisure time than my colleagues had at their disposal. My experience in other countries had opened my eyes to discover the faults of my own, and I felt it my duty to redress them.'

"The populous town of Düsseldorf, not far from Kaiserswerth, had a large prison, the inmates of which were shut out not only from society, but also from all religious instruction. The young minister obtained permission from the Government to preach every alternate Sunday afternoon to the Protestant portion of the prisoners. His first sermon to them was preached on the 9th of October, 1825. 'My chapel,' he wrote, 'was not very inviting : two sleeping-rooms with the bed-straw piled up in a corner, and a doorway between them, where I stood, that I might be heard by the women on one side and the men on the other.'

"A society for prison reform was now established, after the English pattern ; and those horrible jails, which hitherto had been filthy dens and scenes of the lowest immorality, were gradually turned into places fit for the habitation of human beings, besides being provided with sufficient means for making the inmates better members of society.

"Pastor Fliedner was the heart and soul of the society. And in order still further to qualify him for what was to be his life-work, he undertook a second visit to Holland in 1827, and another to England and Scotland in 1832. Here he made the acquaintance of Elizabeth Fry, of Dr. Chalmers, and of many others gifted with rare talents for rescuing perishing men.

"He felt that he was ready for his work now, and looking up to God, he put his hand to the plough, never to loosen his grasp till death stiffened his fingers. An asylum for discharged female convicts was the first thing wanted. People laughed at the idea of such a class remaining in a house, the door of which would be open all day. Fliedner's excellent wife, who, from love to the lost and the neglected, taught some years in the reformatory of Düsselthal, joined him with all her heart. Their little garden-house was given up for the purpose. This happened in 1833. The next year the garden-house was too small. A larger place was procured, and friends sent in their contributions for the work. But the garden-house did not remain empty. The little children of the factory people were invited to fill it during the day. A good girl, a member of Fliedner's church, offered her services as teacher. She began a knitting-school, which in 1836 was enlarged into an infant-school for poor children of all denominations, organized after the pattern of Wilderspin's Infant-School at Spitalfields.

"But now the sick people were to have their turn. An hospital was what was wanted,—an hospital under the control of Christian love and the care of Christian nurses. A large house was for sale. Fliedner had no money, but he bought the building. On the day of payment some good friends advanced the required sum. But the whole town was astir when it was known that the premises were to be converted into an hospital. Fliedner, however, allowed the people to talk, and did his work, and the work proved the best answer to all their complaints.

"But no sooner was the hospital set agoing than the want of fit nurses was felt. And where were they to be got? Of course there were nurses at the different hospitals, but what sort were they? They were mostly persons who, after having failed at every other employment, had taken to sick nursing as a last refuge from starvation. Fliedner perceived that an institution for training females as sick nurses was urgently wanted. Gertrude Reichardt, the first Christian young woman who entered Fliedner's deaconess-house, was the pioneer of a numerous band of servants of God scattered over the world, who in self-denying love and humble patience devote their lives to the nursing of the sick, the instruction of prisoners, the education of children, and the consolation of the poor and the afflicted.

"An asylum for discharged female convicts, an infant-school, an hospital, a deaconess-house—those four little seeds were sown in humility and weakness, in fear and trembling, but not unaccompanied with the voice of fervent prayer which rose up to God day and night. And God heard that prayer and gave the increase, and spread His protecting hand over the tender little plants, so that they could defy the summer's drought and the winter's frost.

THE DEACONESS-HOUSE AT KAISERSWERTH.

" When," says De Liefde, "in November, 1864, I visited the Kaiserswerth Establishment for the second time, and stood by the newly made grave that contained the mortal remains of its great and deeply-lamented founder, I was so struck with astonishment at the wonderful work which God, through the instrumentality of a weak human being, had performed, that I regretted I could not stay six months at the place, and write a special volume about what my eyes saw and my heart enjoyed.

"I entered one of the two main entrances of the building, and found myself in a simple flag-paved hall or passage. A woman guided me across a spacious garden to a row of buildings which ran parallel with the main establishment. One of these humble buildings is the dwelling of Mrs. Fliedner.

"A deaconess guided me through the whole establishment. It took me three hours to walk over its extensive premises, and to take a peep into the principal apartments. At length, passing through a beautiful garden, we arrived at the *Feier-Abend Hause*—a beautiful symbolic name for a 'House of Rest' for old deaconesses. *Feier-Abend* means the evening which precedes a great festival.

"The various buildings of the Colony of Kaiserswerth are ranged in six groups, between which are spacious and well-laid-out kitchen and flower gardens.

" First comes the chief building, the so-called Mother-House, which contains the dwelling-rooms and bed-rooms for the deaconesses, the hospital for male and female invalids, the apothecary's room, the writing-room, etc. At present 415 sisters are connected with this establishment, of whom 171 are probationers. They are divided into two classes,—*Nursing* and *Instructing* Sisters. The former attend to the various wards, and are, in the men's wards, assisted by men-nurses. The latter, of whom there are 31, with 43 probationers, are trained for educational work. During the year 1863 not less than 789 invalids were nursed, of whom 260 were Roman Catholics and eight Jews. Protestant as the Institution is, yet free admission is granted to the Roman Catholic priest to visit the members of his Church, and to administer extreme unction to the dying. Nor does the presence of Romanists hinder the mission-work which deaconesses, under the direction of the Chaplain of the Establishment, carry on among the sufferers. All the invalids, no matter what denomination they belong to, hear every day the Gospel read and explained. And every annual report contains touching instances of the conversion of individuals, who entered the Hospital in a state of ignorance or infidelity, and either left it or died, rejoicing in the God of their salvation.

" The Instructing Sisters are again divided into classes, viz., Teachers of Infant Schools, and Teachers of Girls' Schools, and other educational establishments. When sent out to teach, two of them always go together, "in the same manner as the Lord sent out His disciples, so that they may strengthen one another mutually in their weakness.' They exercise themselves in the practice of teaching at the Infant School of the Establishment (which is attended by from seventy to eighty children), at the Orphan house, at the Town school, or at the Children's wards in the Hospital, and they receive their theoretical training at the Seminary, which is a spacious three-storied building with thirty-six windows in front.

"The view from this house is very picturesque, having gardens on one side, and the Rhine on the other. Of the pupils who are trained here only a few are Deaconesses, as most of them prepare themselves for independent situations. At the close of 1863, out of eighty-five pupils who were in the house, only twenty-two were Deaconesses. The total number of teachers trained at this Establishment since its commencement, amounts to 1007, who are scattered throughout the world, conducting hundreds of schools, from those for more advanced girls down to those for infants. It is gratifying and often touching to read the letters in which these teachers give an account of their work to Dr. Fliedner. And the testimonies to their usefulness borne by Christians who live in the districts where they are laboring, are very strong.

"The Infant school is the third building which attracts our attention. Certain recent alterations and repairs have made it an excellent and well-ventilated school-house. A large playground gives plenty of opportunity for recreation to the seventy or eighty children who here receive instruction every day. One of the Deaconesses is the chief teacher. Assisted by a male teacher, she instructs her younger Sisters in Infant school management.

"Next comes the Female Orphan Asylum, which receives girls under twelve, who have lost one or both of their parents. They are not poor, but of rather respectable families, and are mostly daughters of clergymen and schoolmasters. This house is at the same time intended to be a kind of training school for future Deaconesses. Ten of the present Kaiserswerth Deaconesses were trained at this Orphan House. The present number of pupils is twenty-seven.

"The oldest of the Kaiserswerth institutions is the House of Refuge for released Female Prisoners and Magdalens. Since its foundation in 1833, 439 girls, either discharged prisoners or fallen women, have been received, and, after a residence of one or two years, provided with suitable situations. The present number of inmates is thirty.

"The Institution for Protestant Insane Women of the educated class is a magnificent building, situated in a pleasant garden. It contains forty rooms of various sizes, besides bath rooms, halls for social meetings, and musical entertainments, passages for walking exercise, a covered arcade used in wet weather, and a green house which affords an opportunity for gardening, even in winter. The medical direction of the House is in the hands of the Hospital physician, and Pastor Disselhoff attends to the spiritual treatment of the unhappy inmates. The physician and the pastor are assisted in their work by eighteen Deaconesses. Of the fifty-five ladies who were discharged during the last three years, sixteen were perfectly cured, eleven were much improved, eleven were sent back uncured to their families, and twelve were removed to other establishments. During the year 1863 the House contained forty-one inmates, of whom twenty-six were suffering from melancholia.

"I have already mentioned the House of Rest. But not only are the aged Deaconesses cared for, there is also a place of retirement and refreshment for those who require rest and change of air. It is Salem, a pretty-looking farm-house near Ratingen, seven miles from Kaiserswerth, situated at the foot of the woody hills through which the beautiful stream of Anger flows. Here, in the midst of most charming and picturesque scenery, where in summer the fragrance of field and forest soothes the mind, and the freshness of mountain air invigorates the system, the Deaconesses have an opportunity of regaining the health which they have lost through their arduous labors at the sick-beds and in the schools of the poor. It is a true Salem, a house of peace for the weary, who here, in the company of their Sisters, spend some time in quiet communion with Him from whom they derive all their strength for the holy work they have devoted themselves to. A small Filial-orphan House, as it is called, is also connected with this Establishment, and is under the superintendence of two Deaconesses.

"Another Orphan House was founded at Altorf, near Pless, in Upper Silesia. It owes its origin to the typhus which raged in that district in 1848. The noble Count and Countess von Stolberg, residents of Pless, impelled by compassion for the orphans of those who fell victims to the epidemic, gave a building for their use, and put it under Fliedner's direction. The Government also sent a number of orphans from the neighborhood, to have them trained in it as farm-servants. About a yearly average of eighty children have been sheltered, fed, clothed, and trained, at this excellent house of charity.

"So much for the institutions of Kaiserswerth. And now, if we turn our eyes to the North, the South, the East, and the West, we will see not less than 96 stations, where 293 Deaconesses are laboring under the direction of the Committee.* Of these stations 78 are in the kingdom of Prussia, 7 in other German States, 4 in other European countries (at Constantinople, Bucharest, Florence, and Geneva), 4 in Asia, 1 in Africa (Alexandria), and 1 in America (Pittsburg). Eighty-six of them are Institutions belonging to corporations, societies, or communities, whom the Committee has agreed to supply with Deaconesses. Forty-four of these Institutions are hospitals, or infirmaries; 11 schools; 5 poorhouses; 2 orphanages; 2 Protestant homes for maid servants; 2 Deaconess-houses : 1 a school for the blind; and one a prison. The rest are local home-missions, carried on by churches, which employ Deaconesses as their agents. Most of these churches have 2 Deaconesses in their service. In some of the hospitals from 3 to 6 Deaconesses are employed; and at the new Charity House at Berlin there are 8 Deaconesses.

"During the Schleswig-Holstein War 28 Deaconesses were engaged day and night in the hospitals at Gottorf (in the town of Schleswig), Apenrade, Hadersleben, Kolding, and Flensburg.

---

* The Committee bears the name of "Direction of the Rhenish-Westphalian Society for training and sending out (*Beschaftigung*) Evangelical Deaconesses." It consists of eight members. Dr. Fliedner was its vice-President and Secretary.

That such able and zealous sick nurses would be invaluable, every one can understand. They were like consoling angels to the wounded Danes, as well as to their own countrymen. One day General Wrangel visited the Hadersleben hospital, where the Deaconesses had daily to tend from sixty to seventy invalids.

"He here saw a Danish prisoner, with whom he conversed, through an interpreter, about the way in which he was taken prisoner, etc. 'And are you content with the treatment here?' the General asked. 'Content! content!' cried the Dane, in broken German, passionately rising up in his bed, and allowing no time for employing an interpreter: 'Ay, ya, ya, General, thank, thank!' 'All right, my son,' the old General replied; 'but let these Sisters, not me, have your thanks.' And with these words he cordially shook hands with the Deaconesses.

"The hardships and privations which these faithful friends of the sufferers sustained were not few. At Kolding, in Jutland, they had to wage a regular war with mice and other vermin. On one occasion a Deaconess was summoned to some distant place at the dead of night. She flung her mantle round her shoulders, and took her seat in the post-chaise. At daybreak the coachman told her that she could not well go on in that strange dress: her mantle had no back, the mice having eaten it away.

"The Kaiserswerth Deaconesses kept up a cordial correspondence with their colleagues, the Deaconesses of Copenhagen, who were ministering to the Danish army. During the armistice two of them accepted an invitation from their Copenhagen Sisters to favor them with a visit. The queen, having heard of their arrival, kindly invited them to the palace, and expressed to them her gratitude for the care and love which they had shown to her wounded subjects.

"Besides the six Institutions at Kaiserswerth, ten of the above-mentioned stations are under the direct control of the Committee as affiliated Institutions. These are:

"1. The Deaconess Educational School at Hilden, in Rhenish

Prussia; with seven Deaconesses. 2. The Protestant Home for maid-servants at Berlin, with which an Infant School and a School for older girls are connected ; with fourteen Deaconesses. 3. The Protestant Home for Maid-servants at Derendorf, near Düsseldorf ; with four Deaconesses. 4. The Orphan House at Altorf ; with six Deaconesses. 5. The Deaconess Educational School at Florence, with six Deaconesses. 6. The Deaconess Educational School at Smyrna ; with twelve Deaconesses. 7. The Deaconess House at Jerusalem ; with one Deaconess. 8. The Hospital at Alexandria ; with five Deaconesses. 9. The Orphan House at Bairouth ; with 7 Deaconesses. 10. The Boarding School at Bairouth ; with four Deaconesses.

"The Deaconess Educational Schools are of a high class. I visited that at Florence in 1863. It is kept in a fine, large house, which has a beautiful and extensive garden attached. The property belongs to Madame Eynard, of Geneva, who, in the most liberal manner, allows the use of it rent-free. I never saw better accommodation in a first-class boarding-school. There are a great number of large and well-ventilated apartments in the building, which has room for fifty boarders at least. As it was but recently opened, there were only thirteen ; but in the day school there were sixty out-door pupils. Six Deaconesses give instruction in different elementary branches. For French, Italian, English, music, etc., the first teachers of the town are engaged. German is taught by the Deaconesses themselves. The importance of such a first-rate Protestant School in the centre of Roman Catholicism cannot be easily overrated. The solidity of the training and teaching is so generally acknowledged, that pupils from various countries and of all creeds come to the school. While abstaining from anything like direct doctrinal lessons, the Deaconesses carry on their educational labors on a thoroughly evangelical basis. The Bible is *the* Book in all the classes, and the rule for the family-life in the house. Nor is the secular teaching in the least sacrificed to the religious. I was present at a lesson in German literature which the chief Deaconess gave to the first class. One of Schiller's masterpieces was read, and the pupils examined upon it; the pronunciation was so correct, that I could scarcely believe the readers to be Italians; and even a young Greek lady gave such answers to a few questions which I put to her as I could hardly have expected from a first-class pupil in a German academy.

"If abundance of contributions be a proof of popularity, then the Kaiserswerth Institutions are exceedingly popular. Their list of donations and subscriptions for 1863 contains sixty-six closely-printed pages, each of two columns. These gifts are chiefly from Rhenish Prussia and Westphalia, being the two provinces in which the greater number of the Deaconesses are laboring, and in which the Government permits annual collections to be made at the houses and in the churches. In this list there are only four donations from London, of £6 2s. in all, and one from Edinburgh of £15. The King heads the list with an annual subscription of 50 thalers (£7 10s.); above which sum none of the annual subscriptions go. The greater part of them are under one thaler (3s.); and such an annual gift as fifteen or twenty thalers rarely occurs. The donations, of course, show higher figures. Still they do not go beyond 400 thalers (£60), which sum occurs twice; and there are whole columns which do not go beyond one thaler. This seems to prove that the Kaiserswerth Institutions are mainly popular among the lower and middle classes. Even out of the 400 donations that were from Berlin, only 77 go higher than one thaler; and of these the greater number do not exceed two thalers. Still, notwithstanding the comparative smallness of these gifts, the donations amounted to a little above 12,000 thalers (£1800), and the subscriptions to a little under 3000 (£450). The annual collection at the houses and in the churches yielded £650. The Deaconesses earned £1490 by their services in the hospitals and private families, and this sum, after the deduction of £1012 for pocket-money, left a balance of £478. The whole income of the Establishment amounted to a little above 55,000 thalers

(£8250), which was 4672 thalers (£700) less than the expenditure.

"In the income table a sum of 5618 thalers (£843) is set down as accruing from the sale of books and engravings. There is a small publishing business in connection with the Establishment. Its publications amount to between fifty and sixty, large and small, and excel by their amazing cheapness, as well as by their thoroughly evangelical and popular character. Among them a monthly journal, started sixteen years ago and called 'The Friend of the poor and the sick,' (*Der Armen- und Krankenfreund*), ranks foremost. Its price is one shilling a year, and it is conducted by Pastor Disselhoff. It is ably written, and gives full information about the work of the Deaconesses in particular, and also regarding the social and religious condition of the people, and mission-work in general."

Service for the Ordination of Deaconesses,

as used at Kaiserswerth, Prussia.

HYMN.

O, glorious Prince of Life, defend
Thy poorhouse here on earth ; extend
To it Thy shielding care, and deign
That here be never done in vain
The smallest work of love ; and fill
Each soul with strength to do Thy will.

And oh, let Mary's spirit blest
Alike on every Sister rest,
That they in hope, through grief and pain,
May bear Thy yoke and count it gain ;
And if oppressive it should be,
Say to their hearts, "Come, follow Me ;

For I am with Thee—I am He
Who bore the Cross on Calvary."
Then with fresh courage we'll arise,
Pursue our journey to the skies,
Fight for the home we have in view,
And following Thee, our foes subdue.

As Thou Thyself in days gone by,
Supported uncomplainingly
In silence and in gentleness,
And in a spirit full of peace,
For us the yoke of love,—impart,
We pray Thee, Lord, to every heart,

That peace which worketh full of love
And wearies not : grant this, to prove
That Thou art in us and that we
Even on earth are still with Thee.
O Lord, our Saviour, and Defence,
We seek no earthly recompense.

But be our home Thy mercy-seat,
And we shall tread with willing feet
Our pathway here, and striving still
Our lowly duties to fulfil,
Stand waiting for that harvest bright
Reserved for those who walk in light.

ADDRESS.

WE are to-day assembled in the presence of our Lord to celebrate a holy solemnity, to make a solemn but joyful covenant. In order fully to understand the deep meaning of this ceremony, let us imagine ourselves standing amongst the first members of the Church of Christ at Jerusalem —that model of all Christian churches upon earth—just founded by the Apostles, walking in the fear of the Lord and filled with the consolation of the Holy Ghost.

Here, in this newly-planted garden of the Lord, when the number of the disciples was multiplied, were felt those wants and weaknesses which exist everywhere on earth. There were widows and orphans, poor and sick members, who required daily assistance, but whose needs were overlooked for want of regular care. Then the twelve called together the multitude of the disciples and commanded them to choose out seven men of good report, full of the Holy Ghost and of wisdom, to assist the widows and orphans, to take care of the sick and poor, as servants of the Church, or deacons. They then prayed and laid their hands on them and ordained them to the office of deacons.

Not long after the Church, in like manner, appointed female assistants, to provide for the wants of the sick and the poor, as servants of the Church, or deaconesses. The Apostle speaks with praise of Phœbe as of one in the service of the

Corinthian Church, who had been a succorer of many, and of himself also. (*Rom.* xvi. 1.)

These Deaconesses labored after the Apostolic times for many centuries profitably in the Church of Christ. Their charity embraced the poor, the sick, prisoners and children; and in the fourth century forty were active in the Church at Constantinople.

To-day these seven women before us desire to be appointed to a similar work of love in the service of the Church, as those forty,—as Phebe in Cenchræa, as the seven deacons in Jerusalem. They are of good report, as those deacons; they have prayed for the Holy Spirit and the wisdom from above (*Acts* vi. 3); they hold the mystery of the faith in a pure conscience (1 *Tim.* iii. 9); for, feeling their own impurity and sinfulness, they have turned with penitence to the Saviour of sinners, and He has made known to them the covenant of grace, and purified their hearts by faith. They have also been proved, as St. Paul required of the deacons (1 *Tim.* iii. 10); they have gone through a long period of probation, that we might see whether they were skilful and unblamable in the service of the sick and poor

(1 *Tim.* iii. 10); they have, under the direction of the Superior and the physician, exercised themselves in the bodily care of the sick and poor, whose servants they are to be; and under the direction of the Clergyman learnt to satisfy the spiritual wants of those under their care, as far as is consistent with their office. Whenever they could, they have relieved the afflicted and miserable, and have diligently followed every good work (1 *Tim.* v. 10).

Having been found worthy to fulfil the duties of Deaconess, we will to-day, in the name of the Holy Trinity, admit them to this office.

But it is fitting, my dear Sisters, that here, in the presence of God and this congregation, the duties to which you are about to devote yourselves should again be laid before you.

You are to be servants of the Church of God as Deaconesses, especially as ministers of her sick and poor, but also, if need be, of prisoners and destitute children: it will therefore be your duty, according as you shall be specially directed, to serve in a threefold capacity, as

1. Servants of the Lord Jesus.

2. Servants of the sick and poor for Jesus' sake.

3. Servants one to another.

First, as servants of the Lord Jesus. You are not only bound, as every Christian, to live to the honor of God, but you have also made it the special object of your life to serve Him with all your powers in the sick and weak members of His body. You are, therefore, so much the more bound to die to all the pleasures, honors, riches and joys of the world; to seek your joy in this service of love through gratitude to Him, Who took upon Him the form of a servant and suffered death for you, even the death of the Cross.

You are not to seek for abundant earthly reward in this service : if you have food and raiment you must be therewith content.

You must not seek honor from man ; you must go forth unto Jesus, bearing His reproach.

You must not seek earthly pleasure and ease ; you must deny yourselves, and take up your cross daily and follow Him.

What an honor is yours ! You are to minister to Him whom it is the highest honor of the holy angels to serve—the King of kings and Lord of lords,—to serve Him as His handmaid, to wait upon Him in His members.

As Mary of Bethany had always before her eyes the one thing needful, and therefore rejoiced to sit at Jesus' feet, but was also ready, when it was permitted her, to wait upon and to anoint Him—as she did not shrink from expense, trouble, or the derision of men—so must you always desire on the one hand to *hear* Jesus, and on the other to *serve* Him with a love which "beareth all things, believeth all things, hopeth all things, endureth all things." Then will His glorious promises be yours. He will say to you, "I was naked and ye clothed Me; I was sick and ye visited Me; I was in prison and ye came unto Me." "Whoso receiveth a little child in My name receiveth Me." "Come, ye blessed of My Father, inherit the Kingdom prepared for you from the foundation of the world." (*St. Matt.* xxv. 36, 34.)

Secondly, as servants of the sick and poor, for Jesus' sake. As St. Paul made himself servant unto all that he might gain the more, so must you be especially servants of the sick and poor, not to obtain praise from them, but out of love and submission to the Lord whose, representatives you are.

Therefore you must not serve them with such indulgence as might strengthen their perverse will, but always with the holy zeal of parental affection, striving to win their souls for the Lord.

Thirdly, as servants one to another. It is your duty, my Sisters, when several of you are working together, to show that love which leads us in lowliness of mind to esteem others better than ourselves. (*Phil.* ii. 3.) Whosoever will be great among you, let her be the servant of all. If you are one by a living faith in our common Lord and Saviour, you are more nearly related to one another than if you were united by the closest ties of blood. You are acknowledged as daughters by the Great High-Priest, who says to you: "By this shall all men know that ye are My disciples, if ye love another." (*St. John* xiii. 35.)

As such Christian servants, it is your duty,

Finally, with childlike obedience, to respect the authority of the superiors of the Deaconess-institution, who are over you in the Lord, and labor among you with parental love.

In the presence of God and this congregation, I now demand of you, Are you determined faithfully to fulfil these duties belonging to the office of a Deaconess, in the fear of the Lord, according to His Holy Word?

¶ *Answer, Yes.*

May Jesus Christ, the Chief Shepherd and Bishop of your souls, seal your profession, and vow with His Yea and Amen, and own you forever as His. *Amen.*

Draw near, and give me and the Superior your hands in confirmation of your promise.

¶ *Kneel down.**

The triune God, God the Father, Son, and Holy Ghost, bless you and make you faithful unto death, and give unto you the crown of everlasting life. *Amen.*

Let us who are here assembled and desire for these Deaconesses salvation and blessing, pray for them. "O come, let us worship and fall down, and kneel before the Lord our Maker."

¶ *The congregation kneel.*

Father of mercy, who hath led these Thy servants to Thy Son, so that they have given them-

---

* The Deaconesses are ordained with imposition of hands.

selves up to Him for His own possession, and desire to serve Him with all the powers of their body and soul in administering to the sick and poor; we humbly beseech Thee, be merciful unto them and direct their hearts into Thy love, and into the patient waiting for Christ, that they may live and work in Thee and rejoice in Thy favor always.

O Lord Jesus, Thou merciful High-Priest, who hast purchased these souls with Thy blood, Thine they are, they have devoted themselves to Thy service. Enlighten them with the bright beams of Thy truth, strengthen the weak by Thy power, and give them an abundant measure of Thy meekness and humility, that they may acknowledge themselves unprofitable servants before Thee, and desire to be and do nothing of themselves, but only to the honor of Thy glorious Name.

O God the Holy Ghost, Thou Spirit of peace, replenish them with Thy peace, that they, as Thy messengers, may bring peace to the homes and families of the sick, and the circle of Sisters; grant that they may be ever adorned "with the ornament of a meek and quiet spirit," and may be so governed by the spirit of obedience towards all their superiors, feeling that in performing their commands they are obeying Thee. (*Heb.* xiii. 17 ; 1 *St. Pet.* ii. 13 ; 1 *Cor.* xiv. 34.)

Grant them to know, O triune God, that they serve Thee, and not man. Pour out Thy peace upon them like a river (*Isa.* xlviii. 18.) Let Thy free Spirit sustain them, that they may always feel that it is good for them to be in Thy service, and that godliness hath the promise of the life that now is and of that which is to come.

And when duty calls them afar off, go Thou with them, as Thou didst with Jacob. Keep them by Thine angels in all their ways, lest at any time they dash their feet against a stone : lead them with Thy Fatherly hand, guard them by Thy watchful eye, that when they walk through the dark valley they may not fear, and in the hour of death clothe them with the white garments of Thy Righteousness (*Rev.* iii. 5), and give them palms of victory in their hands (*Rev.* vii. 9), and grant unto them the Crown of Life, (*Rev.* ii. 10). *Amen, Amen.*

HYMN II.
Before the celebration of the Holy Communion.

Lord, let them of those five be found
Who when they hear the joyful sound
   Of Thy return, shall bear
Their shining lamps, and on that morn,
To greet Thy Second Advent's dawn
   With joyful hearts prepare.

O Lord, we make our prayer to Thee,
That faith and hope and charity
   May all their hearts inspire.
O Thou, of every light most bright,
Before Whom darkness turns to light,
   Quicken each good desire.

Preserve their souls in faithfulness,
Come quickly, heal, renew, and bless,
   Grant that each hour may be
So counted blessed, Lord, as Thine,
That some good deed in each may shine,
   Each day be given to Thee.

EXHORTATION.

Ye have now entered as servants of Christ into His vineyard : to you is entrusted the joyful duty of ministering to your Saviour in His sick and weak members. Arise, then, arise, my Sisters, gird yourselves as the wise virgins, for His service. Behold the Bridegroom cometh, go ye out to meet Him, with your lamps in your hands. He standeth at the door, and knocketh ; in the form, indeed, of a servant, in the sick and miserable around you. Open then unto Him (*Rev.* iii. 19), feed Him in the hungry, clothe Him in the naked (*St. Matt.* xxv. 40), receive Him in His little ones (*St. Matt.* xviii. 5), visit Him in the prisoners, bind up His wounds in the sick, and accompany Him in the dead to His last resting-place.

Yours is a blessed office, but one also beset with difficulties. How soon will the hands become weary and the knees feeble (*Isa.* xxxv. 3). Yet, thanks be to God, ye know the Bridegroom of your souls, when He comes to you in other form than that of a servant; ye know Him as the Lord of Glory, who anoints with the oil of gladness of His Holy Spirit. Therefore have ye desired this feast of mercy. Ye say, I have need to be fed of Thee, and comest Thou to me?

And lo, He is here, the King of Glory, and saith, "Come unto Me, all ye that labor and are heavy laden, and I will refresh you." Then He, the Bridegroom, standeth in glorious Majesty. He desires to adorn you with His wedding garment—to give you Himself and all His Divine power, in the Communion of His Body and Blood; and ye have well done that ye are come. All things are ready. Open, then, your hands, your mouth, your heart, and receive of His fulness, grace for grace (*St. John* i. 16). Yea, taste and see how gracious the Lord is. Blessed is the man that trusteth in Him.

¶ *During the administration, is sung:*

O Christ, Thou Lamb of God, Who takest away the sins of the world : have mercy upon us. O Christ, Thou Lamb of God, Who takest away the sins of the world : have mercy upon us. O Christ, Thou Lamb of God, Who takest away the sins of the world : grant us Thy peace. *Amen.*

THE THANKSGIVING.

CONCLUDING HYMN.

Source of all bliss and joy divine,
My deepest love, O Lord, is Thine.
To feed, to clothe, to solace Thee,
O Saviour, this is granted me.

When in true thankful love we bear
The poor man's burden, grief and care,
These words to us are sent from Thee,
Come, O ye blessed, unto Me.

All those who little children love,
Whose tender hearts with pity move
For ev'ry sufferer here below,
For the lone captives in their woe.

Those who behold the poors' sad tears,
And still their weeping and their fears,
To them a bright reward Thou'lt be,
A shield, a guard, a panoply.

With heavenly fire then fill each heart
O Jesus, and to us impart
Still more of love, until it be
Our highest, chief felicity,
On earth to minister to Thee.

¶ *Then the blessing is sung:*

The grace of our Lord Jesus Christ and the love of our God, and the fellowship of the Holy Ghost, be with us all. *Amen.*

II. QUESTIONS FOR SELF-EXAMINATION.

The following is a series of questions for self-examination, prepared with especial reference to Deaconesses, by Pastor Fliedner. He has arranged others for those who are preparing to receive the Holy Communion.

INTRODUCTORY REMARKS.

In order that the Sisters may become better prepared to perform their earthly duties to the honor of our Lord Jesus Christ, and more fitted to receive the heavenly treasure (*Rev.* ii. 17), we have arranged some questions for self-examination, which they are required to ask themselves, in the presence of God, at least once every week.

QUESTIONS FOR SELF-EXAMINATION FOR DEACONESSES AND PROBATIONARY SISTERS.

Kneel down, my Sister, in silence and deep humility, before the Holy God, Who is a judge of the thoughts and intents of the heart, and pray thus with David : " Lord, Thou searchest me out and knowest me; Thou knowest my downsitting and mine up-rising ; Thou understandest my thoughts afar off. Thou art about my path, and about my bed, and searchest out all my Ways. For lo, there is not a word in my tongue but Thou, O Lord, knowest it altogether. Try me, O God, and seek the ground of my heart ; prove me and examine my thoughts. Look well if there be any way of wickedness in me, and lead me in the way everlasting.

Thou dost admonish us by Thine Apostle, " Examine yourselves whether ye be in the faith, prove your own selves." O Lord, I must confess with him that I am not sufficient of myself to think *any good thing ;* but do Thou enlighten the eyes of my understanding that I may know how I stand before Thee. And grant Thy blessing to me during this examination, that it may be to Thy honor and my own salvation.

CONCERNING THE MORNING.

1. Did I, on waking, think first of God, with praise and thanksgiving (*Ps.* lvi. 3, 7), or of earthly things?

2. Did I pray for renewed grace and forgiveness, for fresh love, humility and wisdom, to enable me to perform my duty for our Saviour Jesus Christ's sake?

3. Did I omit to mention in my prayers those committed to my care (*Eph.* i. 15–19), the Sisters, those dwelling with me, my relations, my spiritual pastor, and all others who are set in authority over me?

4. Did I pray that I might all the day do everything as in God's sight, seeking the approbation of my Saviour, not desiring to please men?

5. Did I rise punctually and dress quickly, with due regard to propriety and neatness, but without ministering to vanity?

6. Did I in silence collect my thoughts and prepare myself for the united morning devo-

tions? Did I unnecessarily omit them? Did I join in them with my whole heart, and seek to make them profitable to myself?

Concerning External Duties.

7. Did I take care that the rooms intrusted to my charge should be at the proper time swept, arranged, aired, warmed, etc., and when I had to provide for the bodily wants of others, did I do so kindly and faithfully?

8. When I had to nurse the sick, did I endeavor to be present at the visits of the physician? Did I carefully listen to his directions, and conscientiously follow them?

9. Did I take care that those intrusted to me obtained wholesome and sufficient food, according to his directions? and if this was not the case, did I hesitate to give information in the right quarter? Did I, as far as I was able, prevent those intrusted to my care from eating too much, or forbidden food, or becoming in other ways spoiled or pampered?

10. When I had to attend upon the sick or poor children, did I care for their bodily wants, for order and cleanliness, and lead them, as much

as possible, to maintain this, and to employ themselves in suitable and useful occupations?

11. Have I myself industriously endeavored to learn such occupations,—*e. g.*, needle-work, gardening, etc., as well as simple surgical operations?

Concerning Spiritual Duties and Teachings.

12. When I had to assist those intrusted to my care at their devotions,* did I carefully prepare myself for it, and seek to make it edifying and instructive to them, and not keep them too long?

13. When I had to take care of and give instruction to children or other pupils, did I carefully prepare myself beforehand, and impart it faithfully, looking up to God? Did I watch over them as much as possible during their school hours? Have I endeavored to train their hearts and souls aright, and sought to bring them up in the nurture and admonition of the Lord? (*Eph.* vi. 4.)

14. Have I endeavored to make him who has

---

* As it is not the custom in Germany generally to use forms of prayer, the Sisters have to pray without a book.

the care of their souls, acquainted with their spiritual wants, and as far as I could, sought pastoral counsel to assist me in training them religiously, and acted upon it?

15. Have I procured for them, as far as it was in my power, a sufficiency of spiritual food,—*e. g.* religious books, but above all the Bible, and tried to direct them so that they might read profitably?

16. Have I sufficiently sought to cheer and gladden my sick children,—*e. g.* by taking walks with them, singing, telling tales, playing, and so on,—teaching them to rejoice in the Lord alway? (*Phil.* iv. 4.)

17. Have I led them to sanctify Sunday and holy-days, and spend them profitably for their souls, as well during Divine service as before and after; and in doing this, sufficiently considered the circumstances of each?

Concerning my conduct to the Sisters and Superiors, and others.

18. Have I endeavored to show sincere love to those living with me, especially to the Sisters, that we might be of one mind in the Lord? (As

St. Paul admonishes Euodias and Syntyche. (*Eph.* iv. 2). Have I allowed "the sun to go down upon my wrath" (*Eph.* iv. 26), or sought Christian reconciliation before going to rest? (*Eph.* iv. 31, 32.)

19. Have I always been obedient to the Sisters immediately set over me, as well as to my other superiors, with child-like submission, without murmuring or complaining to others, according to the admonition of St. Paul? (1 *Thess.* v. 12, 13 ; 1 *St. Pet.* ii. 13, 16). Have I allowed any feelings of bitterness or anger or dislike to arise in my mind towards those who blamed me? or if such arose, did I immediately recognize their sinfulness, strive to overcome them, confess them to the Lord and earnestly beseech Him to give me a kind and affectionate *heart?*

20. If any duties which had been imposed upon me seemed too difficult or unsuited for me, did I first mention this to the Sister immediately set over me? and if I thought she treated me unjustly, did I complain of her treatment to the other Sisters, and judge her uncharitably? or did I for the time being endure the evil with a meek and quiet spirit (according to the Apostle's ad-

monition (1 *St. Pet.* ii. 19), and then seek redress from those still higher in authority.

21. Have I concealed anything from my superiors which I was conscientiously or by the rules of the house bound to tell them immediately, whether it related to myself or others, or the institution.

22. If other Sisters have been placed under my care, that I might direct them in their work or receive assistance from them, did I always treat them with kindness, meekness, and humility, as our Saviour teaches us by His example (*St. John* xiii. 2–15,) and by His word (*St. Mark* x. 42–45; and *St. Matt.* vii. 12.) If it became my duty to admonish or punish, have I endeavored to do it always in a spirit of holy love, and as kindly as possible in words and manner, also as privately as could be? (*St. Matt.* xviii. 15, 16.) Did I prepare myself for it by looking up to God, and did I pray for the offender? (*St. James* v. 16.)

23. Has the fear of man, or the desire to please man, led me to be silent when my duty required me to admonish or punish? (*St. Luke* xvii. 3, 4; *Eph.* v. 11; *Gal.* i. 10; 1 *Sam.* iii. 13; *Isa.* lvi. 10; *Prov.* xxvii. 23.)

24. In my work did I look upon my own things instead of on those of others, or seek to impose the difficult and disagreeable duties upon others, instead of rather doing them when I could myself as a servant of the Sisters, for Jesus' sake ? (*Phil.* ii. 3, 4.)

25. Have I kept my tongue in check, avoiding all frivolous and useless gossiping, both with the Sisters, patients, and others residing in the house, and avoided an unsuitable intimacy with the two last classes of persons ? (*St. James* ii. 26.) Have I related things which I ought not, to strangers, about the Sisters ?

26. Have I shown a partial love towards some Sisters, and, on the contrary, repelled others ?

27. Have I remembered in my prayers all the wants of our Deaconess' Institution, and all the Sisters connected with it : also all other similar institutions and missionary societies for the extension of the Protestant Church ?

28. (If stationed far from Kaiserswerth,) have I endeavored to keep up the connection with our parent house, by regular correspondence and reports, by keeping monthly hours, (of prayer,) and following the other directions of the Superi-

ors there, have I tried to excite in those around me sympathy for it?

29. Have I during the time of my service in this part of the Lord's vineyard, endeavored always to maintain a serious, dignified, and reserved behavior, as is becoming a Deaconess of the Lord, and not sought the intimate acquaintance of any man? (1 *Cor.* vii. 34.)

Concerning the training of my own soul, and my improvement in performing the duties of a Deaconess.

30. Do I accustom myself daily to hold communion with the Lord in prayer at other times besides the fixed hours of prayer? (1 *Thess.* v. 17; *Col.* iv. 2; *St. Luke* vi. 9, 13; *St. John* xiv. 13, 14; *Ps.* lxxiii. 28.)

31. Do I diligently read the Holy Scriptures (*Acts* xxii. 11), that they may be profitable to me for doctrine, for reproof, for correction, for instruction in righteousness? (2 *Tim.* iii. 16; *St. John* v. 39; *Ps.* cxix. 10, 5.)

32. Have I been led to acknowledge my sinfulness by diligent examination of my heart and conduct, and with penitent faith earnestly

prayed for forgiveness of my sins and my regeneration by the Holy Ghost, and if not, do I daily pray for it? (2 *Cor.* xiii. 5; *Acts* xix. 2; 2 *St. Pet.* i. 10, 11; *Rom.* viii. 14–16; *St. Matt.* v. 3–9.)

33. Do I endeavor to prove myself a disciple of the Lord Jesus by a constant endeavor to become lowly in my own eyes (as David, as St. John the Baptist and St. Paul, (2 *Sam.* vi. 22; *St. John* iii. 30; 2 *Cor.* iv. 16; xii. 9, 10,) by firmly renouncing the world and its pleasures (1 *St. John* ii. 15, 17,) by purifying myself from all pollution of the flesh and spirit, especially from my favorite sins, by a daily advancing in holiness and in the fear of God (2 *Cor.* vii. 1; *Phil.* iii. 12, 14), and by bringing forth the fruits of the Spirit? (*Gal.* v. 22.)

34. Have I spent the whole of Sunday as the Lord's day, and exclusively in His service? (*Isa.* lviii. 13.) Did I prepare myself for the public service by self-examination, by collecting my thoughts and withdrawing my mind from earthly cares, by reading the Holy Scriptures, that the Lord might open my heart to attend to the things spoken? (*Acts.* xvi. 14; *Eccles.* v. 1, 2; *Ps.* xxvi. 6.) Have I been present at Divine Service

as often as I could, and solemnly pondered what I there heard in my heart? (*St. Luke* ii. 19; *Heb.* x. 15; *St. Matt.* xvii. 20; xxxi. 55; *Acts* ii. 46.) Have I endeavored to spend the time after service for my own bodily and spiritual strengthening and refreshing, remembering to keep holy the Sabbath day?

35. Have I diligently thought on my baptismal vows, and on their renewal in the presence of God at Confirmation? (*Eccles.* v. 3, 4; *Ps.* i. 14, 16, 17.)

36. Has the frequent thought of the sufferings and death of Christ been to me a shield to quench the fiery darts of the wicked one? (*Eph.* iv. 16.)

37. Have I embraced every opportunity of receiving the Holy Communion, endeavored to receive it worthily, and then, as at other times, sought the advice of him who has the care of my soul?

38. Do I seek to enrich my mind with Christian and other useful knowledge, as it is profitable for my office? Do I take advantage of the lessons offered to me, and use all other opportunities of improvement faithfully, to the honor of God? Do I endeavor to do this when I am stationed

far off, and obtain for this purpose advice from the parent house? Do I allow myself to be so absorbed in learning or teaching that it leads my soul rather away from, than to God? Do I seek so to turn all my learning and teaching to His service, that the acknowledging of the truth may lead me to eternal life, that I may grow in grace and the knowledge of our Lord and Saviour Jesus Christ? (*Tit.* i. 1, 2; *St. Pet.* iii. 18; 2 *St. Tim.* ii. 25, 26.)

39. Have I omitted to take care of my bodily health, as it is my duty, by enjoying fresh air at the appointed times, by moderation in eating and drinking, not indulging my appetite, or breaking the rules of the house? (1 *St. Tim.* v. 23; 1 *Cor.* x. 31.)

40. Do I regularly consider the rules of the house and the duties of my office there set forth, and the passages in the Bible upon which they are founded (*Rules for the House*, § 3–5), and my vows as a Deaconess? Do I use these questions once every week?

41. Do I earnestly struggle against all vanity, keeping conscientiously to the prescribed dress, adorning myself with the ornaments required in

Holy Scripture? (1 *St. Tim.* ii. 9; 1 *St. Pet.* iii. 3, 4.)

42. Have I sought to be faithful in that which is least (*St. Luke* xvi. 10), obeying all other prescribed rules for the Lord's sake, however unimportant they may seem, that no loss or injury may occur to the institution which I serve, through my fault? (*St. John* vi. 12.) Do I remember that our institution is only supported by charity, and receive all that is given me with thanksgiving?

43. When not permitted to see the fruits of my labor, have I allowed myself to grow desponding and idle in my work instead of hoping ever against hope, and looking upon myself as a sower who must wait patiently for the blessing from heaven? (*St. James* v. 7, 8), and trusting in God's promises? (*Isa.* xlix. 14; lv. 10, 11; *Ps.* xc. 16.)

44. If God allows me to see the good seed spring up into the hearts of any amongst whom I labor, do I give all the glory to Him Who has given me power and opportunity, and acknowledge myself an unprofitable servant? (*St. Luke* xvii. 10.)

45. Have I in all my actions, even when not actively employed in the duties of my office,

sought to show that I am the Lord's servant, giving offence to none, but rather seeking the honor of the Sisterhood? (2. *Cor.* vi. 3.)

46. Do I daily endeavor to give up my will more entirely to God, forgetting those things which are behind (*Phil.* iii. 13; *St. Luke* ix. 62), forsaking with my whole heart all that I have (*St. Luke* xiv. 33), even all those which were formerly my favorite thoughts and wishes, that they may not disturb me in my holy service, that I may be able to serve the Lord Jesus always with more faithfulness, perseverance, and self-denial, in His vineyard?

47. Do I receive all the sufferings which God sends me, with submission? Do I seek by them to grow in patience, in renouncing my own will in obedience to the will of God? (*Heb.* x. 35, 36; *St. Matt.* xvi. 14, 25.) Do I cast all my care for the future upon Him, knowing that His grace is sufficient for me (2 *Cor.* xii. 9), so that my mind may not be moved from the peace of God and the simplicity which is in Christ Jesus, that I may seek to rejoice in Him alway, and to be careful for nothing, but in everything, by prayer and supplication with thanksgiving, make my requests

known unto God ? (2 *Cor.* xi. 3 ; *Phil.* iv. 4–7 ; *St. Matt.* vi. 31–34.)

48. Is it my joy to be dead indeed unto the world, to walk by faith, having my life hid with Christ in God ? (*Col.* iii. 1–3 ; *Gal.* ii. 20.)

49. Is my aim in every thought and deed to advance the glory of God and my own salvation, as well as that of others, so that I am able to say " to me to live is Christ, and to die is gain"? (*Phil.* i. 21.)

III.

EXTRACTS EROM RULES FOR DEACONESSES.

Any person who wishes to become a Deaconess* must be able to read well, write, and know something of arithmetic. She must be eighteen, and usually not above forty. She must express her wish in writing to the directors, and send with it—

1. A certificate of Baptism.
2. A short account of her life, composed by herself.

---

* Many more educational qualifications are required of those who are to be especially trained for Teaching-Deaconesses in the Training School.

3. A testimonial of good moral character from her pastor.

4. A medical certificate of good health.

She must obtain the consent of her parents, if living.

Every Deaconess must go through a probationary period of from six to twelve months: this time shall be extended, if it seem desirable, to two, or even three years. It is to be spent in the institution. The probationary Sister is expected to perform cheerfully all the work imposed on her, and in a docile spirit to receive all the instructions and directions given her.*

When she becomes a Deaconess she receives a salary of £3 15s. ($18.30.)

A Deaconess is not received unless she be elected by a majority of those then residing in the house.

Some special Duties of the Sisters.

To observe punctually the directions of the doctor with regard to medicine, nursing, and

* The Sisters are encouraged to make use of the library, and to take every opportunity of obtaining such instruction as may improve their minds and assist them in their work; e. g. to study foreign languages, and singing. A museum of natural history is in progress.

diet, lighting, warming, etc., without speaking against his advice, and to inform him daily of the patient's state. To make use of no remedies but those prescribed by him. To send for a clergyman as soon as the patient desires it. To read to those of their own communion the Bible or other edifying works, according to the direction of the clergyman. To pray with him, and if the clergyman desire it, to inform him of the patient's state of mind.

The Deaconess must endeavor to perform all her duties without noise. She must be kind, cheerful, patient, and watchful, so that it may appear she serves the sick for Christ's sake. In her spiritual care of the sick she must endeavor to point out to them the love of God—that though He woundeth, His hands make whole (*Job* v. 18); that He allows us to suffer in the flesh that we may cease from sin (1 *St. Pet.* iv. 1); that He makes whole, that we may sin no more (*St. John* v. 14); and that the works of God may be made manifest in us. (*St. John* ix 1–3.) She must consider her patients as those who, by means of their cross, are placed in Christ's school; she must be kind and patient, yet not always speak only of God's grace, but when necessary, warn and exhort to listen to the awakening voice from above.

"Those whom I love I rebuke and chasten; be watchful, therefore, and repent." (*Rev.* iii. 19.) Especially, she must strive to promote Christian resignation to God's will, that the patients may not vex themselves with anxious thoughts about their recovery, or worldly cares, but may cast all their care upon God, in everything by prayer and supplication, with thanksgiving, making their requests known unto Him (*Phil.* iv. 6); caring only for one thing, that they may please the Lord; whether they live, living to the Lord, or whether dying, dying to Him.

The Deaconess must not allow the patients to talk much of worldly things, nor even allow them to converse so much on religious matters, that they have not time for meditation, and communion with God. This would besides be injurious to herself. She must by no means dispute with the sick, nor allow them to dispute with one another about religion. She should employ the patients in useful work, as far as their strength will allow.

Attendance on the sick in the town of Kaiserswerth and other places.

If a Deaconess be required in a family, the Superior shall first visit it and appoint a Sister or Sisters. These Sisters shall not be assisted by relations or friends in their treatment. If any Sister finds her services superfluous she should leave, since her duty is not to amuse or be simply a companion. She shall take her meals alone, or in the patient's room. She must observe a prudent reserve in her conduct to all members of the family, and devote herself entirely to her patient. She must not repeat what she hears, nor allow any gossiping with servants or others. She must not go out except when it is necessary to call the doctor or clergyman immediately. She must not make acquaintance with or visit the neighbors, the duties of her office allowing her no time for it. If change of air be necessary, permission will be granted to the Sisters to stay with relations, or sometimes friends. A Sister is not permitted to receive any presents; should they be pressed upon her, she must send all to the institution, to be placed in the Sisters' box, the contents of which are devoted to Christmas presents, etc., to the Sisters, or journeys for the benefit of their health.

4.
Sisters of Charity of the Society of the Exaltation of the Holy Cross,

St. Petersburgh, Russia.

THE following account of the Sisterhood of the "Society of the Exaltation of the Holy Cross," was prepared a few years since, by the Baroness de Rahden, first maid of honor to her Imperial Highness the Grand Duchess Helen of Russia, at the request of the Rt. Rev. J. Freeman Young, D.D., Bishop of Florida, to whom it was originally addressed. It has been kindly furnished by him for publication, having never before been translated or printed.

"SIR,—I scarcely know how to excuse myself in your eyes, for my long silence since the receipt of your parcel, and of the kind letter which accompanied it. Whatever may have been the numerous reasons which prevented me from answering at once, I do not care to enumerate them, but prefer to throw myself on your indulgence. Permit me to begin by thanking you, in the name of Madame la Grande Duchesse Hélène. Her Imperial Highness was greatly touched by your promptness to serve her, as also by the kindness of the Reverend Dr Muhlenberg. His book affords valuable information with regard to the hospitals, and will remain in the library of the

Grande Duchesse, as a souvenir of the fraternal spirit existing among all engaged in doing good. In exchange for the 'carte,' which Dr. Muhlenberg sent with his work, Madame la Grande Duchesse begs he will accept the enclosed portrait. The other copy is for yourself, as also the photographs of the Superior of our Sisters of Charity, Elizabeth Kartzoff, of the Priest of the Society, Father Constantine Stefanowitch, and of the Physician-in-chief, Doctor Tarassoff. You wished to have some historical notes on the foundation and progress of the 'Society of the Exaltation of the Cross.' I give you them with pleasure, together with the necessary dates and statistics.

"It was the Crimean war which first gave to Madame la Grande Duchesse Hélène, the first idea of the foundation of a charitable society for the purpose of doing hospital and ambulance work on the field of battle. Her Imperial Highness made an appeal to the patriotism and charity of the Russian women, and soon quite a number presented themselves. The Grande Duchesse, assisted by a council of competent persons, presided herself, in the choice of candidates, who should serve an apprenticeship during a given length of time, in order to become accustomed to the arduous duties which would eventually devolve upon them. By means of zeal and good will, the difficulties which constantly arise in the organization of this work, so entirely new in our country, are slowly but surely overcome.

"I recall with much emotion, that time of anguish and enthusiasm, when each endeavored to take his share in the heroic struggle of our country against combined Europe. There was a general spirit of emulation in sending to the army, lint, linen, clothing, medicines, tea, dainties, etc. The palace of the Grande Duchesse Hélène, resembled a large depôt, where were collected together all these pious donations. As soon as there was a sufficient quantity on hand, her Imperial Highness forwarded them to the Crimea, generally under the care of an employee of her own household, who placed them in the hands of the Sisters of the Cross, to be conscientiously distributed in the hospitals.

"But to return to the subject. On the 4th of November, 1854, a first division of Sisters, under the direction of Mme. Stahowitch, the widow of an infantry Colonel, set out for the Crimea, accompanied by a physician, Doctor Tarassoff, and by a priest who was to be to them a confessor. On the 5th of December, of the same year, a second division followed them, under the direction of Sister Baconnino, one of the most devoted heroines of that phalanx of courageous and indefatigable women. Two physicians accompanied them. The Grande Duchesse Hélène employed, at her own expense, during the campaign, five distinguished physicians, specially recommended by the Universities of the country. It would occupy too much space to give the dates of the departures of each of these Societies of Sisters. At the end of the year 1855, they numbered in all, 203, which had gone to the Crimea at Sebastopol, Bakhtchisarai, and Simferofol—at Cherson, Nikolaew, Elisabethgrad, and at Finlande, Helsingfors, Abo, and Wibourg.

"Before leaving, they took a very simple oath, which bound them for one year, and in which they promised obedience to their Superiors and charity toward the sick, for the love of our Lord Jesus Christ. Their rules were contained in a few sentences. The service of God in the persons of the sick and wounded comprised the whole. Their costume, simple, convenient, and scrupulously neat, was an object of special care to the Grande Duchesse, who understood the importance of garments peculiarly adapted to this kind of work.

"The Sisters had dresses of dark brown merino, with a deep cape, white collar and cuffs, and white apron, and a cap of a peculiar shape. A light blue ribbon held the gilt cross, which they put about their neck on the day when they took their vows of service. This cross had on one side the image of the Saviour, with these, his own words: 'Take my yoke upon you,' (*St. Matt.* xi. 29,) and on the other side, these words of the Psalmist, 'The Lord is my strength.' (*Psalm* xviii. 1.)

"As you will have seen, by the letters of the Sisters, and by the report of Dr. Pirogroff, which I gave you when you were in

Russia, the Sisters were placed in the various hospitals and ambulances of Sebastopol, in small divisions, always under the supervision of a Sister Superior, while the Superior-General had the entire executive government of all the divisions. I will not dwell in detail on the services rendered during the war by the Sisters of Charity. The grateful army cherishes a tender recollection of it. Our celebrated military surgeon, Dr. Pirogoff, who was their immediate chief, and to whom the Grande Duchesse Hélène had especially entrusted the direction of the community in the hospitals, awarded to them the most glorious testimonials. This extraordinary man, whose medical genius was only equalled by his high integrity, passed seven months in the hospital at Sebastopol. His most faithful ally was the Sister Raconnine, who remained on duty until the very last moment, and did not cross the bridge, which was almost immediately afterward destroyed, until the very last of her patients had been conveyed to a place of safety. After the taking of the tower of Malakoff, commenced the work of transporting the sick to Simferofol, and to Bakhtchisarai, while the hospitals of these two cities sent all their sick and wounded, who could be moved, to Nikolaeff, Ekaterinoslaw, and other cities of the Empire. Only those who understand the dreadful condition of the roads of the peninsula, can appreciate the difficulties—I might almost say martyrdom of these transportations, in the months of October and November. Four times the Sister Bacounine, and the nine Sisters under her, accompanied hundreds of the wounded from Simferopol to Ekaterinoslaw, often walking beside the carriages, wherein the wounded were stretched out, bathing their wounds evening and morning, and distributing warm drinks among them from time to time.

"It was just at this time that illness and death came among the communities. The first Superior-General, fatigued in body and in mind, had set out on her return to St. Petersburg, with several of the Sisters, also worn out with their labors, after a year of hard work. Another Superior-General, the Sister Kartzoff, had taken her place, and governed the community with a rare intelligence. At Simferopol, the Sister Kartzoff found herself at the head of the hospitals where the typhus fever was raging. The ardor of the struggle was no longer sustained by the hope of triumph. The inclemencies of a rainy autumn followed the tropical heat of summer—devastating fever had succeeded to the somewhat lesser sufferings of the wounded. A renewed amount of energy and determination was requisite on the part of the Sisters, but their strength was not equal to their courage. The Superior-General was the first to fail. This irreparable loss left in the community a gap which nothing could ever fill. Then the Sister Kartzoff was removed for many long weeks by malignant typhus from her post of duty. The Sister Baconnine also narrowly escaped death. However, her iron constitution gained the mastery, and it was to her that the Grande Duchesse entrusted the post of Superior-General. Eleven of the Sisters lie at rest in the Crimea, among the brave soldiers whose death agonies they had helped to soothe. Two of the Sisters died in Finland during the war. 'Blessed are the dead which die in the Lord. They rest from their labors, and their works do follow them.' (*Apocalypse* xiv. 13.)

"After the peace, as fast as the hospitals were organized in the south, the Sisters set out again for Petersburg, some to return to their families, some to devote themselves forever to the care of the poor and the sick. The groundwork of the Grande Duchesse, though temporary originally, was destined to take deep root throughout the country. One band of Sisters (31) adopted voluntarily the doctrines of the Grande Duchesse, with regard to the future permanency of the Community. Her Highness allowed them to occupy one wing of her palace, while they were awaiting more permanent arrangements, and applied at hospital head-quarters, in order to obtain for them appointments to a new field of activity. As in all countries of the world, there was a strong opposition to the introduction of Sisters into the hospitals. Through the influence of the Grande Duchesse they were, however, *tolerated* in one of the hospitals —one of those least cared for by the city, that of the working people, where the mortality had been greatest, typhus fever almost continual, and the administration almost wholly neglected. Their rough apprenticeship during the war had been of advantage to the Sisters, and they went to work with great zeal. At first only tolerated, they soon became indispensable—the laundry as well as the kitchen was the object of special care, and the hospital underwent an entire change. At the end of two years, the Sisters were as much loved and respected, as in the hospitals of the Crimea, and they themselves are so much attached to the hospitals, that, notwithstanding their arduous duties, they feel it a privilege to remain there.

"Is it not a lasting glory to human nature to witness the increase of zeal, in proportion to the emergencies of the case. Already the Minister of the Marine, under the enlightened influence of the Grand Duke Constantine, had willingly opened to them the gates of his hospitals (in 1856). The Grande Duchesse Hélène established them in the Child's Hospital (in 1858), and in Maximilian's Hospital (in 1857), which are under her jurisdiction. Finally the Minister of War called meetings of them (in 1862), and continued to do so. The insurrection of Poland (in 1863), rendered it necessary that some of the Sisters should be sent to the western provinces of the Empire. At Wilna (in 1864) the government had entrusted to them the care of the Foundling Hospital. At the time of which we write, the Sisters were thus divided—at the first grand Hospital at St. Petersburg, seventeen Sisters and one Superior. At the Marine Hospital at St. Petersburg, six Sisters and one Superior. At the Workman's Hospital at St. Petersburg, eight Sisters and one Superior. At the Maximilian Hospital, two Sisters. At the Child's Hospital, one Sister and two novices. At the Hospital for Women, or Mothers' Home, one Sister, and all the novices in rotation. At Wilna, in the Foundling Hospital, three Sisters. The ambulance, in the Mothers' Home, the school, visiting the poor at their homes, and the various duties of the establishment, occupy the remainder of the Sisters, who number in all sixty-one, with nine novices. These last necessarily vary in number, from time to time.

"After having paused at the temporary establishment of the Community at the Palace Michel, we must first follow it to a rented house, at Cail, where it remained for a period of two years, and thence to a house which the Grande Duchesse Hélène secured for the Sisters of Charity, and which they occupied after July, 1859. Situated between two of the most thickly-inhabited districts of the city, the Mothers' Home of the Society of the Exaltation of the Cross, is eminently adapted as the abode of the Sisters. In fact, their field of usefulness, at first limited to the care of the sick and wounded in the military hospitals during the war, has by degrees extended itself over an almost unlimited area. The principle established as the basis of rule by their august founder is this,—that all human suffering, which appeals to charity, comes within the sphere of duty of the Sisters. This very broad principle necessitated a wise moderation in the execution of duty, or, if I may so express myself, a central concentration. It was resolved that the care of the sick poor should always be of the first importance, either in the hospital, the ambulance, or the dwelling. The care of sick who were able to pay is absolutely forbidden, except in very extreme cases. In the care of the sick is naturally comprised visitation of the poor at their own homes, and the necessary duties pertaining thereto, as well as the visitation of hospitals for workmen, and asylums for old men. After this come the schools and homes for orphans, prisons, etc.

"I speak only of what comprises the field of activity of the Sisters. It is very probable that it will not become materially extended, though attaining larger proportions in the various branches; but if any unforeseen trouble should arise, the assistance of the Sisters would be at once solicited, unless directly forbidden by their rules. At this very time, for example, when the epidemic which has spread among our working classes, has made many orphans, without homes or support, the Society of Sisters, moved to pity by the sight of these little forsaken creatures, applied to the Grande Duchesse Hélène, and with her assistance, and that of the benevolent Society of St. Petersburg, a temporary asylum for orphans is about to be established, under the direct care of the Superior. Servants of the poor, for the love of Jesus Christ, they give food and drink to those who hunger and thirst, they clothe the naked, nurse the sick, and visit those who are in prison, without distinction of age, faith, or nationality.

"The Mothers' Home serves as a dwelling for the Sisters who have an office among the Community. Such are the Sister Superior, the Sister Econouse, the Sister Maitrosse, the Nuns, the Sisters charged to visit the sick, the Sisters of the school, the Sisters who direct the hospitals for women and for children, the Sisters who do the work of the hospital for workingmen, the Nuns, and the old, infirm Sisters. The maison mère, supplies as charity, a Woman's Hospital, of fifteen beds, opened in 1860. It is in this hospital that the nuns serve their apprenticeship, of the care to be given the sick. A Child's Hospital of twelve beds,* a school for twenty little poor girls, and an ambulance, of which I will speak more in detail.

"Since the beginning of their labors in the hospital for workmen, the Sisters had been struck with the serious condition, often almost desperate, in which the sick arrived at the hospital. Wounds in the leg, so frequent in certain trades, was neglected even to mortification, rotting of the bones, or even fatal fevers—in a word, the sufferers struggled until the very tools fell from their hands, before they would give up, and go to the hospital. To the remonstrances of the Sisters, the patients replied that they could not give up work just for a slight wound or temporary ailment, and yield to others the post wherein they earned their daily bread. What could be answered to this argument? The Sisters had the happy idea to make these workmen promise to return to them to be cared for, in case of returning illness, and they could nurse them. They

---

* The Grande Duchesse is about building a child's hospital, of eighty beds, beside the Society of the Cross.

promised to dress their wounds, and to ask advice from the doctors of the Society in case of illness. Soon, two or three persons presented themselves to the Society. It seems that the authorization given was a blessing, for the number of the sick increased day by day. Doctor Tarassoff, a true brother of charity, devoted an hour each morning to the little ambulance which was almost imperceptibly formed. A room on the ground floor was devoted to the dressing of wounds. At the end of the first year, forty or fifty persons came every morning. And soon Doctor Tarassoff was no longer equal to the emergency. The Sisters and novices, in turn, dressed the wounds, and prepared the medicines, which the Grande Duchesse Hélène gave gratis.

"The charity of the Sisters had succeeded. The working population ran in crowds to the Society of the Exaltation of the Cross. It became necessary twice to enlarge the apartment devoted to the ambulance. And now, four large rooms, receive every morning and evening hundreds of persons, in need of care, who arrive from all parts of the town. Eight doctors, two of whom are more especially surgeons, examine the patients, and write the necessary prescriptions. Small operations are performed in a room devoted to this purpose; the patients who require several hours of rest, find a bed in a separate room, where they can remain temporarily. A bathing apparatus is connected with the ambulance—in fact every effort has been made to furnish to the patients every requirement out of the regular order of things. The medicines are prepared in the pharmacy of the Community, by a Sister and her aids, and given gratis.

"In 1861, 8000 persons, and even more, passed through the ambulance; in 1862, 14,000, in 1863, 19,400, and 1864, 23,000. The Municipality de Petersburg, struck by the immense amount of good wrought by this institution, has voted an annual subscription of five thousand rubles, to pay for medicines, and remunerate the physicians. From nine o'clock in the morning, the court of the Society is full. With a patience and an abnegation worthy of all praise, the doctors remain at their post until the last patient has been attended to. They often do not leave until three in the afternoon. The Superior herself, the Sister who superintends the Women's Hospital in the Mothers' Home, and all the Nuns, except those who are on duty, devote their whole mornings to assisting the doctors. What an apprenticeship for the Nuns, before being admitted to the service of the hospitals! What a school of practice for the doctors! What a blessing for the poor! The example also has done good.

"Another ambulance has been established, under the care of the philanthropic society, in a central part of the city. I must still tell you of the government of the Society, and its rules. The rules are elaborated, so to speak, every day. Besides the fundamental principles, which are few and simple, practise has built slowly, but surely and safely, the walls of the edifice. Little by little, they have fixed what life itself only outlined, and after ten years, they now arrange, sort, and regulate definitely what is, without written law, the rule of the House. Naturally, terms of admission have been determined since the first. During the war, the candidates took the dress of the Sisters, and received the Cross after a short experience of three or four months. The term of novitiate service varied from six months to a year. During this time the novices are only employed in the Mothers' Home, where they are initiated in all that pertains to their vocation. The mistress of the Nuns, one of the oldest Sisters, overlooks and directs them. To enter the Society, they must be between eighteen and forty years of age—of blameless character, good health, and knowing how to read and write. After a year of service, which may be prolonged, at the pleasure of the Council, the Novices take the dress of the Sisters.

"A religious ceremony, invoking the blessing of God on the new Sister, accompanies this decisive act. In taking the dress, each Sister promises one year of service—this promise is renewed every year, for five years. At the end of this term, the

Sisters receive the Cross, and do not renew their promise, for it is understood that unless from very urgent causes, a Sister who holds the Cross, will never of her free will leave the service. It is in a very solemn manner that the Sisters receive the Cross. They receive the sacrament the same day, or the day previous. All the assembled Society assist in the religious act, by which the priest, in giving them the Cross, consecrates in the name of God, the voluntary sacrifice of their lives. No vow binds them —the love of Christ and of their neighbor, alone, holds them.

"After the Crimean War, persons of all creeds entered the ranks of the Society. With an elevation of thought, worthy the Christian Church, the rules still allow this. Catholics and Protestants are equally welcome in the Society. Naturally, religious life there, is purely orthodox. Morning and evening prayers, divine services, pious lectures, follow each other with regularity, under the spiritual guidance of the priest or confessor of the Society. Except the prayers morning and evening, the Sisters of this persuasion are not obliged to attend. I have never heard a complaint of religious difference. To understand such a remarkable state of things, it is necessary to appreciate fully the spirit of inborn toleration which characterizes the Russian people.

"The true toleration, is a more perfect phase of the development of the Christian idea, in the world. Toleration of faith, resembles mildness in strength. It is the serene expression of an unshaken confidence. By the nature of things, the number of Protestant and Catholic Sisters has greatly diminished since the society no longer offers purely patriotic motives. In the course of its six years' existence there were two or three conversions from Protestantism to the orthodox faith. Beside the reasoning persuasion of the Sisters—which it does not belong to me to judge—the communion of prayer, the external influence of an imposing form, have naturally affected their minds. I believe that in the long run, unity of faith will assert itself more and more, without apparent effort.

"It is even likely that in a few years, the Society will consist only of orthodox Sisters; but no narrow, legal rule, will exclude Christian souls of good will, belonging to other faiths. The Superior governs and directs the Society—and to her, all the different branches of the Society report. She decides upon the order of service, and all interior details; it is she who communicates with the authorities to whom are subordinate the divisions of Sisters, established in the hospitals. Nevertheless, all matters pertaining to the Society in general; all reception or dismission of Sisters, all expenses, however slight, could not be decided by her, without the aid of the Council. The Council is presided over by a lady chosen by the Grande Duchesse, and represents all the exterior interests of the Society—the controller of its books and accounts, the defender of its rights and its people of business, relative to the ministers with whom the Society is in relation. The members of the Council are, the Superior, the Priest of the Society, the Doctor, and all the Sisters who have an administration to direct, because they represent certain interests, which they are required to report, and to protect against the central power. The resolutions of the Council are submitted to the Grande Duchesse, and sanctioned by her, before going into effect. Up to the present time, the Grande Duchesse Hélène has named the Superior and the officers, but it is now strongly proposed to introduce an elective principle, by right of which the Superiors will be elected every three years. The original Superior, Elizabeth Kartzoff, is the Sister of the Chief staff-officer of our army in Caucasus. At the head of the Society, since 1860, she combines, with a rare experience, an administrative talent quite exceptional, absolute devotion to her vocation, and great simplicity. She is the guide and example of the Sisters—always the first at work, and the last to rest. The mode of nominating the Priest and the medical authorities is not as yet definitely arranged. The Grande Duchesse is very much occupied with these questions. She desires to leave with the Society she so dearly loves, a sound organization, and so well arranged that it can, after her death, go on steadily and independently, secure in the public esteem and public gratitude. Much remains to be done—much to be thought of—nothing must be hastily done in so important a work; no detail, however small, must be neglected.

"I have put before you the life of the Society as concisely and harmoniously as I could. Let it not be supposed I am blind to the many imperfections of the work I love. I would neither deny nor hide them. They often sadden and discourage the Sisters themselves, but when I reflect on all that the Society does, and all its merits, I say with the prophet of the Old Testament, "Blessed is the man whose strength is in Thee; in whose heart are the ways of them. Passing through the valley of tears, they dig them a well; they go with strength to appear before God. (*Ps.* lxxxiv. 5, 6, 7.)

"I end this long letter, dear sir, as I began it, with the expressions of sentiments of high esteem, and sincere sympathy, with which I am ever devotedly yours,

"EDITH DE RAHDEN."

St. Petersburg, March 10-22, 1865.

ALMIGHTY GOD, the giver of all good gifts, who, of Thy Divine providence hast appointed divers Orders in Thy Church; give Thy grace, we humbly beseech Thee, to all those who are to be called to any office and administration in the same; and so replenish them with the truth of Thy doctrine, and endue them with innocency of life, that they may faithfully serve before Thee, to the glory of Thy great Name, and the benefit of Thy Holy Church; through Jesus Christ our Lord. *Amen.*

www.ingramcontent.com/pod-product-compliance
Lightning Source LLC
Chambersburg PA
CBHW020324240426
43673CB00039B/912